BLACKBUARD STRATEGIES

OVER 200 FAVORITE PLAYS FROM
SUCCESSFUL COACHES FOR
NEARLY EVERY POSSIBLE SITUATION

Great American Media Services • Sparta, MI

Published by Great American Media Services,
P.O. Box 128, Sparta, MI 49345
For additional copies or information on other books or publications offered by Great American Media Services, write to the above address.
Telephone: 616-887-9008 Fax: 616-887-2666
Email: whcirculation@winninghoops.com
www.winninghoops.com

Manufactured In The United States of America

FOREWORD

I'VE HEARD hundreds of coaches say there aren't many secrets left in the game of basketball. Any coach worth their whistle knows that in order to win games your players must consistently execute the fundamentals: passing, cutting, screening, shooting and defense.

Every now and then, a coach needs a special play:

- A sideline out-of-bounds play against pressure.
- A quick hitter after a timeout or at the start of a quarter.
- A baseline inbounds play against a zone or an open look for a three-pointer late in the game.
- A play that can change the momentum of the game in your favor.

Blackboard Strategies is that extra coach on the sideline. These plays are the best plays submitted by winning coaches and come directly from many years of exciting Blackboard plays in *Winning Hoops*.

The Blackboard section has always been one of my favorites. In every issue of *Winning Hoops* I receive, it's the first thing I turn to. Coaches from every level of the game sharing their most successful ideas, what could be better? I've successfully used plays I've read about in my own games.

There may not be any secrets left in the game, but at least you'll be left with a few tricks up your sleeve after studying all of these game-winning plays. *Blackboard Strategies* is a great book, one that coaches from grade school through college should find useful.

—Steve Smith,
Head Coach,
Oak Hill Academy,
Mouth of Wilson, Va.

KEY TO DIAGRAMS

① **Player with the ball is circled**

$\rightsquigarrow$ **Dribble**

X **Defensive Player or player in line during drill**

$\longrightarrow$ **Cut**

$\longmapsto$ **Screen**

--→ **Pass**

NOTE:

THE SCHOOLS LISTED AFTER EACH COACH'S NAME ARE THE SCHOOLS EACH WAS WORKING AT WHEN THE PLAY WAS ORIGINALLY SUBMITTED FOR PUBLICATION IN *WINNING HOOPS*.

SINCE THE COACHING PROFESSION IS VOLATILE BY NATURE, MANY OF THE COACHES HAVE SINCE MOVED TO NEW POSITIONS OR RELOCATED.

CONTENTS

SPECIAL TIP

SECRET TO INBOUND PASSING

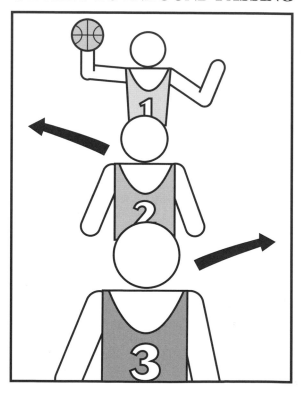

When your team is inbounding, let the ball signal the direction the players should move. Have the inbounds passer hold the ball up with one hand and slap it with the other before the pass. This signals player 2, who always goes to the ball side, to move as indicated in the diagram. Player 3 goes to the oppo-site side. This visual cue eliminates guesswork by the inbounds passer, thus allowing for earlier inbound passing.

—Dean Hollingsworth,
Rockdale Hill School,
Rockdale, Texas

Chapter 1

SIDELINE OUT-OF-BOUNDS

SIDELINE THREE-POINT PLAY

This is a special-situation play that will allow you to get the ball to your best perimeter shooter or afford an interior player a chance to score inside.

It is best to have the ball positioned within 10 feet of the top of the circle along the sideline. This gives the best angles for both passing and screening.

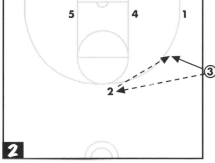

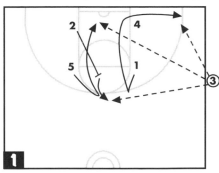

DIAGRAM 1: 1 fakes toward mid-court, reverse pivots quickly and cuts underneath 4 who is positioned on the ball side block. If 1 gets the pass, they can either shoot or post feed to 4.

At the same time, 5 fakes toward the middle of the court to create space as 2 steps up to back screen 5's defender. 5 spins and cuts hard to the basket.

If 2's defender switches, a mismatch is created and most likely offers a chance for the lob pass.

After 2 has screened for 5, 2 will step out for a direct pass from 3 and shoot the jump shot.

DIAGRAM 2: Depending on how the defense will defend 3, the inbounder is often the most dangerous threat to score after the ball has been put into play. Here 3 steps inbounds and receives a quick return pass form 2 for a shot.

—Tom Reiter,
Washington and Jefferson College,
Washington, Pa.

SIDELINE THREE-POINT PLAY

DIAGRAM 1: From this set, 2 breaks toward the basket.

DIAGRAM 2: 1 breaks toward the ball.

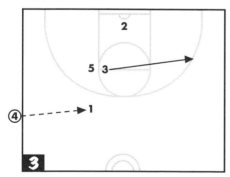

DIAGRAM 3: 4 passes to 1 and 3 breaks to the wing.
DIAGRAM 4: 1 dribbles over while 4 joins 5 to set a double screen for 2, who pops out to the wing beyond the three-point arc.

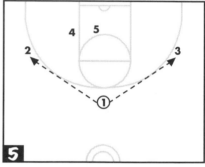

DIAGRAM 5: Now 1 has the option of passing to 2 or 3 for the three-point shot. 3 can also look to 5 under the hoop for an inside shot.

—Steve Smith,
Oak Hill Academy,
Mouth of Wilson, Va.

SIDELINE OUT-OF-BOUNDS PLAY

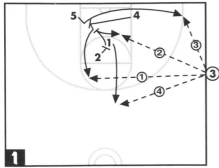

This play, which has been very successful for us, gives the inbounds passer (3) four options.

Option 1: Pass to 4 near the foul line after 4 sets a screen for 5.

Option 2: Pass to 2 in the lane area coming off screens set for 1 and 4.

Option 3: Pass to 5 going to the corner off 4's screen.

Option 4: Pass to 1 at the top of the key off 2's screen.

—Bill Agronin,
Niagara University,
Niagara, N.Y.

OUT-OF-BOUNDS: 4 OPTIONS

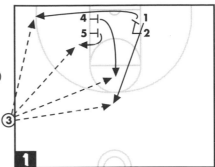

This play from the side out-of-bounds gives you four scoring options. After players are set in a double-stack formation, the following moves take place, in order: 2 picks for 1, who comes hard to the top of the key. 2 then breaks hard to the ball side corner off a double pick set by 4 and 5. 4 then rolls to the foul line. 5 turns and posts up hard; if 5 is fronted, you've cleared the back side for a lob. Four options are now available to 3. 3 can pass to either 1 or 2 for the three-pointer, or to 4 or 5 for the two-pointer.

—Dave Canter,
University of Tennessee-Chattanooga,
Chattanooga, Tenn.

SIDELINE INBOUNDS PLAY VS. MAN-TO-MAN

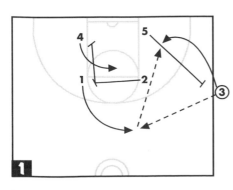

2 sets a pick for 1, who comes off the pick to receive the inbounds pass from 3. After 2 sets the pick, 2 screens again for 4, who comes off that screen and cuts to the middle of the lane. After 3 inbounds to 1, 5 sets a back pick for 3. After receiving 3's inbounds pass, 1 looks for 5's back pick for 3, then feeds a back door pass to 3.

—Jon Pye, Central Missouri State,
Warrensburg, Mo.

SIDELINE OUT-OF-BOUNDS

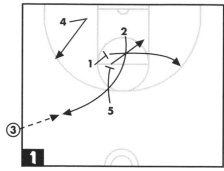

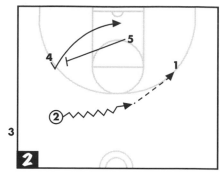

DIAGRAM 1: 3 prepares to inbound. 1 and 5 screen down for 2, who comes to the ball. 1 fills the opposite-side wing. 4 sets their defender up, then comes to the ball.

DIAGRAM 2: 3 passes the ball into 2, who dribbles and passes it to 1. 5 back picks for 4, who cuts to the ball.

—John Gibson,
University of Tennessee-Chattanooga,
Chattanooga, Tenn.

SIDE OUT-OF-BOUNDS WITH 4 OPTIONS

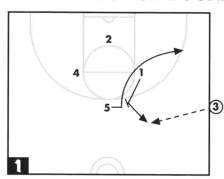

DIAGRAM 1: 3 inbounds the ball. 1 back screens for 5; 3 looks to hit 1. **DIAGRAM 2:** With the ball in 1's hands, 4 down screens for 2 (your best inside/outside combination) and 5 holds for a count, then screens for 3. Timing is key because 1 must scan his options from left to right—first 2, then 4, 3 and 5. Not everyone will be open at the same time.

—Will Rey,
Loyola University,
Chicago, Ill.

SIDELINE PLAY IN OFFENSIVE END

This play is very effective when you need a two- or three-point shot.

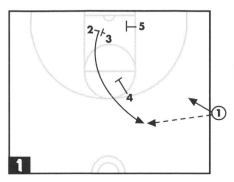

DIAGRAM 1: To start the play, 3 screens down for 2, who cuts high off a second screen set by 4. 1 looks for 2 high for a three-point shot. (A variation might be 2 starting high, then cutting low off 5's screen and 3, then going high).

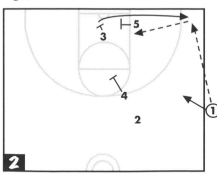

DIAGRAM 2: After 3 screens for 2, 3 cuts low off a baseline screen by 5. 3 can either shoot the corner jumper or dump it inside to 5 locked low.
DIAGRAM 3: If the ball is passed to 2, 4 screens down for 5, who curls hard inside. 2 can dump the ball inside to 5. 1 always steps in and spots up for a return pass. This play can also be used with zones; players just screen the

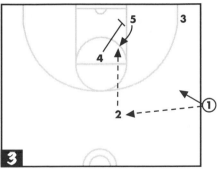

zone and spot up. After all the cuts are made, you have an overload situation.

—Tom Moriarty,
Hartwick College, Oneonta, N.Y.

SIDELINE ENTRY EIGHT PLAY

5 screens diagonally for 1, who comes hard to the ball. 4 releases to the ball in case 1 does not get open. On the entry pass, 2 screens for 3, who cuts to the basket and continues to the weak side off the baseline screen by 5. After setting a back screen for 3, 2 opens up and steps behind the arc.

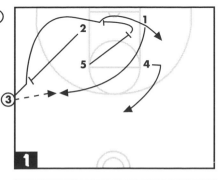

—Rick Berger,
Westfield State College,
Westfield, Mass.

SIDE-OUT

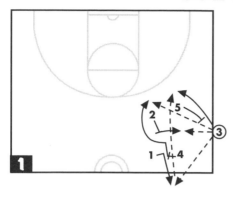

This play features four options.

OPTION 1: 4 sets a screen for 1, then 2 immediately sets a screen for 4. 3 then lobs to 4.
OPTION 2: 3 passes to 1, who comes off 4's screen. Then 1 passes to 4 moving toward the basket.
OPTION 3: 3 passes to 1, who passes to 3, who is coming off 5's screen.
OPTION 4: 3 passes to 2, who is a safety option.

—Nate Webber,
McCorriston Catholic High School,
Trenton, N.J.

SIDELINE INBOUNDS VS. MAN-TO-MAN

This play works best against teams that really get out and deny the ball inbounds. 2 takes a position one stride off the sideline, with just enough room for one player to fit between them and the sideline. 4 is three or four strides behind 2. 5 posts at the mid-lane and 1 is about 6 to 8 feet up court from 2.

for 1 to use. We sometimes even have 2 face the timeline rather than the sideline. If 1 gets the ball off this cut, you have a potential two-on-one with 1 and 5. The third look is a lob to 2 off the screen from 4. This option is seldom open, but it keeps the defense occupied long enough for you to get the ball to your safety valve—the 4 man rolling to midcourt.

—Jim Blaine,
Benton High School,
Benton, Wis.

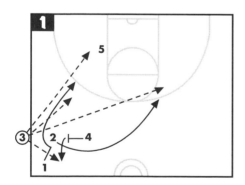

The first look for the inbounder is to 5. If 5 is one-on-one, you may want the ball to go straight in to 5. The second look is to 1, who runs their defender off 2. 2 does not actually set a screen, but is simply a stationary target

SIDEOUT ISOLATED PLAY

This play is designed to get one of your post players the ball for a quick score.

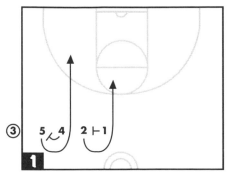

DIAGRAM 1: From a line stack, 5 comes around a quick screen by 4. At the same time, 1 sets a back pick for 2, who quickly cuts toward the basket.

DIAGRAM 2: 4 sets a solid screen for 1, who gets the inbounds pass from 3. Meanwhile, 2 sets a pick for 5 cutting across the lane.

DIAGRAM 3: As 1 dribbles toward the right wing, 2 posts up right above 5, forming two options for the point. If those options aren't open, 4 will be quickly cutting toward the basket, for a third option.

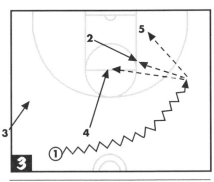

—Brian Hafalia,
Corpus Christi High School,
Daly City, Calif.

SIDELINE BOX SET

This sideline box set can be used to get the ball in play in the backcourt or frontcourt against an aggressive man-to-man defense.

The first option is to look for an easy score after 5 screens for 3, who flies to the basket. At the same time, 4 screens for 2, the safe receiver of the inbounds pass from 1.

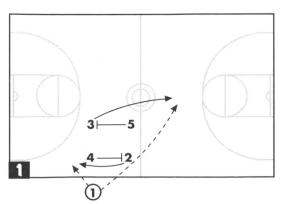

—Bob Sonday,
Monsignor Donovan
High School,
Toms River, N.J.

OUT-OF-BOUNDS PLAY

DIAGRAM 1: 3 comes to the ball off a double screen. 4 acts as the safety valve.

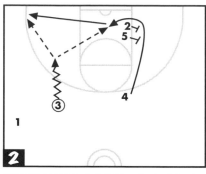

DIAGRAM 2: 3 dribbles the ball looking for 4 coming off the double low-post

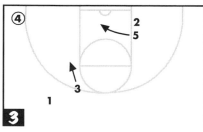

screen. 4 goes to the corner if not open.
DIAGRAM 3: 5 posts hard from across the lane or 4 can take the shot from the corner. 3 can step in for the jump shot and 2 is in rebounding position.

—Rich Ward,
University of Maine-Machias,
Machias, Maine

OUT-OF-BOUNDS PLAY FOR LAYUP

This play, which will work for a layup or a three-pointer, is effective against a

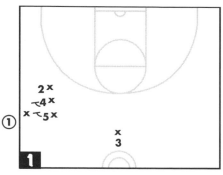

tight man-to-man.
DIAGRAM 1: 4 and 5 set a double screen for 2. 3 stays near half-court as

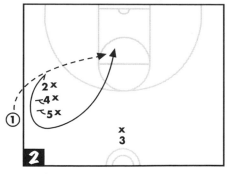

a safety outlet.
DIAGRAM 2: 2 jab steps toward the basket, then uses screens set by 4 and 5. Coming off the screens, 2 should be wide open for a lob. If needed, there is an open look to pull up at the three-point line as well.

—Scott Doan,
Florida Christian High School,
Miami, Fla.

SIDE OUT-OF-BOUNDS VS. MAN-TO-MAN

This play is designed to get a good shot for 4, your best inside scorer.

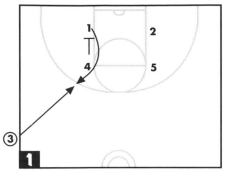

DIAGRAM 1: 4 sets a down screen for 1 who curls around the screen and receives the ball no higher than the three-point line.
DIAGRAM 2: 5 sets a ball screen for 1 at the same time as 2 is setting a screen for 4. If 4 isn't open, you can take the play one step further by having 5 down screen for 2.

—Ricky Norris,
Oak Ridge High School,
Oak Ridge, Tenn.

SIDE OUT-OF-BOUNDS (BOX-SIDE-OUT)

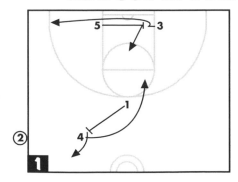

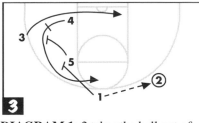

DIAGRAM 1: 2 takes the ball out of bounds. 5 screens for 3, 1 screens for 4. 2 can look for a quick shot, 5 in the lane, 4 rolling to the basket or the safety valve pass to 1.
DIAGRAM 2: If 2 inbounds to 1, 2 immediately slashes through the lane to set up the offense.
DIAGRAM 3: 1 starts the play by passing to 2. 4 and 5 set a double screen for 3. 1 screens for 4 for second option.

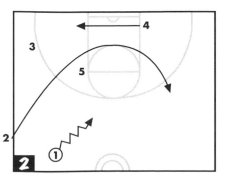

—Nate Webber,
McCorristin Catholic High School,
Trenton, N.J.

SIDELINE OUT-OF-BOUNDS PLAY

This out-of-bounds play is very effective in attacking a man-to-man defense.

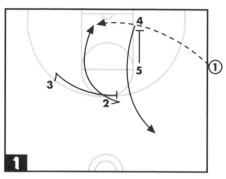

DIAGRAM 1: 5 sets a screen for 4 while 3 sets a screen for 2. 1 can pass the ball directly to 2 under the basket.

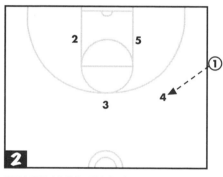

DIAGRAM 2: If 2 isn't open, 1 inbounds to 4.

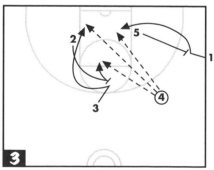

DIAGRAM 3: 1 comes in and 5 sets a

screen for 1. 2 sets a screen for 3. 4 can then pass to 1 or 3 or to 2 rolling into the lane.

—Vinod Vachani,
Welham Girls' High School,
Dehra Dun, India

INBOUNDS "SPREAD"

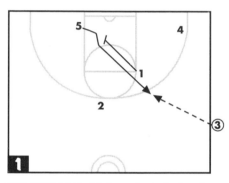

DIAGRAM 1: 3 inbounds to 5 after 1 down screens for 5.

DIAGRAM 2: After 5 catches the pass, 4 up screens for 3 to create a scoring opportunity. 2 screens the screener (1). 2 pops out.
DIAGRAM 3: 3 can also inbound to 1 for a three-point shot.
DIAGRAM 4: 1 can reverse the ball to 2 who hits 3 for the flex cut.

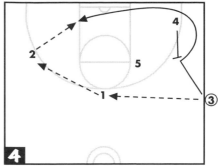

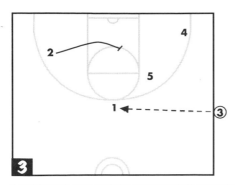

—*Myron Lowery, Harding University High School, Charlotte, N.C.*

BOX PLAY FROM SIDELINE

Set up this box formation with your post players near the ball.

the middle of the lane and posts up.

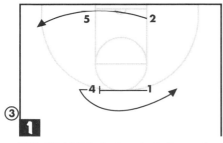

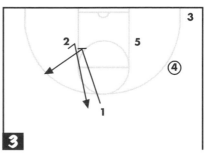

DIAGRAM 1: 3 takes the ball out of bounds. When the referee hands the ball to 3, 2 breaks to the near corner off a low screen by 5. 4 starts toward the ball and loops off a back screen by 1.

DIAGRAM 3: 1 screens away for 2, who comes high for a shot or ball reversal.

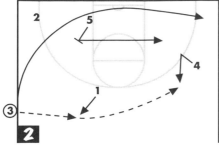

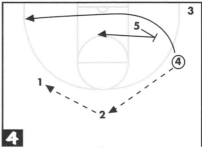

DIAGRAM 2: 1 pops out and receives the ball. 1 reverses the ball to 4 as 3 makes a low cut from out of bounds off a back screen by 5. 5 rolls back to

DIAGRAM 4: If 2 reverses the ball to 1, 5 back screens for 4, who makes a low cut.

—*Tom Moriarty,*
Oneonta High School,
Oneonta, N.Y.

SIDELINE PLAY WITH MULTIPLE OPTIONS

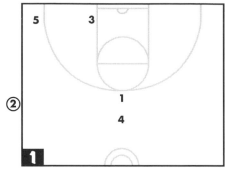

DIAGRAM 1: 2 is the inbounder and a strong three-point shooter. 5 is a good low post player. 3 is a small forward capable of scoring off the dribble. 1 is the point guard, 4 is a power forward.

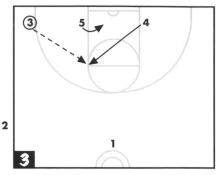

DIAGRAM 3: 3 has possession of the ball in the corner. The first option is a pass to 5, posted on the low block. If 5 is not open, 3 should pass to 4. 4 should look to 5, who cuts across the lane in the high-low game.

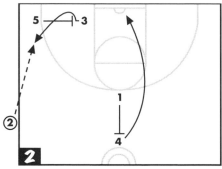

DIAGRAM 2: 1 sets a screen for 4, who cuts hard to the basket. 5 sets a screen for 3, who cuts to the corner behind the three-point line. If 4 is not open for the basket, the pass should go to 3.

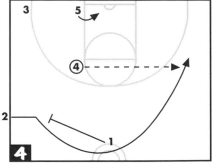

DIAGRAM 4: 4 has the ball at the elbow. As 5 cuts across the lane, 1 screens for 2. 2 cuts hard off the screen to the off-side wing area behind the the three-point line. If 4 cannot pass to 5, the ball should be reversed to 2 for a three-point shot.

—Kenneth Edwards,
Cox High School,
Virginia Beach, Va.

SIDE OUT VS. AGGRESSIVE MAN-TO-MAN

We often get pressured on our sideline inbounds passes. By spreading out along the sideline, if the defense continues to pressure they are forced to play one-on-one without much help. It also opens up the court for drives to the basket.

DIAGRAM 1: 1 should be your point guard (best passer), 5 should be your "go to" player. Stay spread to isolate the defenders.

DIAGRAM 2: If the defender on 5 plays behind, pass directly to 5 for one-on-one to the basket. If 4's defender doubles down, 4 can cut to the basket.

DIAGRAM 3: We can also cut 3 to the basket it the defense is tight or fronting.

DIAGRAM 4: Our final option has 5 dropping to the basket to take their defender deeper in the lane. 4 screens for 3 cutting to the corner. 3 can shoot, pass to 5 or wait and set up the offense.

—DuWayne Krause,
Immanuel Lutheran School,
Marshfield, Wis.

QUICK-HITTING SIDE OUT PLAYS

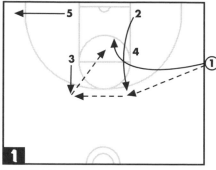

1

DIAGRAM 3: 2 breaks to the corner. 3 pops out high. 5 kicks out to the corner. 1 passes to 2. 4 cuts to the block and receives a pass from 2. 4 posts and scores on the baseline or hooks to the middle.

—Mike Ingram,
Lansing Community College,
Lansing, Mich.

DIAGRAM 1: 2 flashes high off a screen from 4. 3 pops out high to the three-point line. 5 breaks to the corner. 1 passes to 2. 2 passes to 3. 1 runs off a screen from 4 and receives the pass from 3 cutting to the middle.

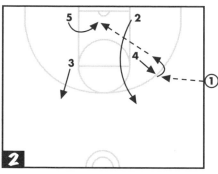

2

DIAGRAM 2: 2 flashes high off the screen by 4, 3 pops out to the three-point line. 4 steps to the ball. 1 passes to 4. 4 turns and passes to 5 ducking in the lane. 5 seals the defender and looks to score.

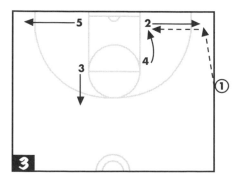

3

THREE-POINT "THRILLER"

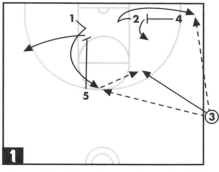

1

We use this play when we have the ball out-of-bounds on the side. It can give us a three-pointer or a quick two-pointer.

OPTION 1: 4 screens in for 2, who pops out on the baseline for a shot. If we need a two-point basket, 4 is also a primary option.

OPTION 2: 5 screens down for 1. If 1 can't shoot after catching the ball, 1 looks to the inbounder (3), who follows the pass for a quick spot-up.

—Gene Keady,
Purdue University,
West Lafayette, Ind.

OUT-OF-BOUNDS PLAY

This play works best when 2 is your best shooter and 4 is your best leaper.

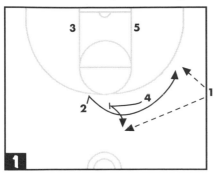

DIAGRAM 1: 4 screens for 2 and then opens up to the ball. 1 passes to 2 if 2 is open or goes to 4, who is opening up to the ball.

DIAGRAM 3: If 2 or 5 do not get the ball, 1 back screens for 4 for the alley-oop and then opens up to the ball.

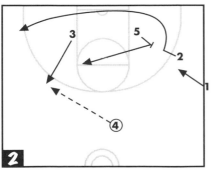

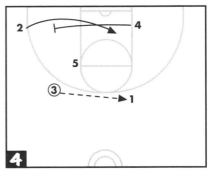

DIAGRAM 2: 4 ball-reverses to 3 while 5 back picks for 2 and then flashes to the ball. 3 looks for 2 in the corner or 5 flashing to the ball.

DIAGRAM 4: If 3 ball-reverses to 1, 4 continues to the corner and sets a screen for 2, who cuts off the screen for a third scoring possibility.

We are now ready to run our motion offense.

—Geoffrey Groff,
Lancaster Mennonite High School,
Lancaster, Pa.

"POST"

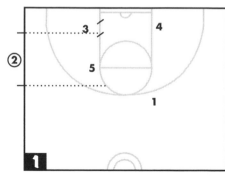

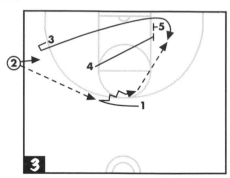

DIAGRAM 1: Have a big guard or forward take the ball out-of-bounds. 5 posts near ball side elbow, 4 on the weak side low post. This play works best when the out-of-bounds point is near the free throw line.

DIAGRAM 3: If 2 cannot get the ball into 4, pass to 1. 4 returns to the opposite low post to help set a double pick with 5. 3 fakes the back screen and cuts baseline using the double screen. 1 passes to 3 for an open shot.

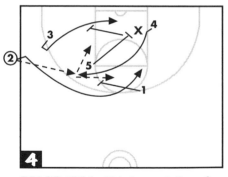

DIAGRAM 2: 5 turns and screens for 4 coming to the ball side elbow for the entry pass. As 4 receives the ball, 3 back screens for 2. 2 cuts baseline for a possible layup. 3 may also be open after the screen for an open jumper.

DIAGRAM 4: This is a variation of the "normal" play. 5 screens for 4 cutting to the elbow, but now 5 sets a second pick for 3. 3 fakes the back screen then turns baseline off the pick from 5. 2 cuts high over 4 and off a screen from 1 for an open jumper. 4 can pass to 3 near the basket or to 2 for the open shot.

—Wim Cluytens,
Mechelen High School,
Mechelen, Belgium

WOLF AGAINST ZONE

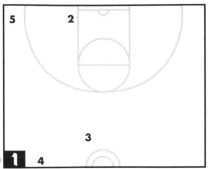

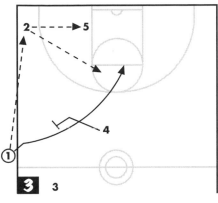

DIAGRAM 1: 1 is the point guard. 2 is the best three-point shooter. 5 is the best low-post player. 4 is the best screener. 3 is a guard or small forward.

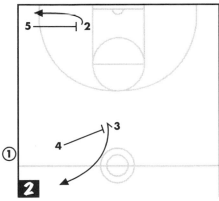

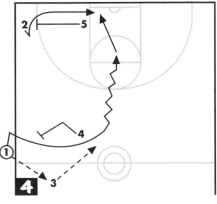

DIAGRAM 2: When the official hands 1 the ball, 5 screens in for 2 and 4 down screens for 3. 2 comes off the screen to the corner looking for a three-point shot. 3 goes to the back court as a safety release.

DIAGRAM 3: If 2 does not have a three-point shot, 2 feeds the low post. It is possible to lob to 5 if 5 is fronted because usually there is no help-side player. 4 back screens 1's defender and 1 cuts to the foul line. 2 can hit 1 for a layup or 1 can hit 5.

DIAGRAM 4: If the ball is inbounded to 3, 4 back screens 1, who cuts to the ball side off the screen. 3 hits 1 driving to the foul line. On 3's pass to 1, 5 back screens 2. 1 can drive for a layup or hit 2 cutting to the basket.

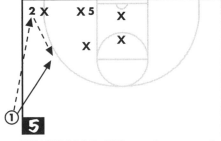

DIAGRAM 5: If 2 gets the pass and does not have a shot or cannot feed 5, 1 simply steps inbounds and sets up for a return pass for a three-point shot against the zone.

—Kevin Sivils,
Runnels High School,
Baton Rouge, La.

WINNING HOOPS...
LIKE HAVING ANOTHER ASSISTANT COACH ON YOUR BENCH!

If you want to win more games, subscribe to this award-winning practical "X's and O's" publication which is jammed with plays, diagrams and techniques for basketball coaches at all levels—from well-known NBA and Division I college coaches to men and women coaching grade school kids as volunteers.

This six-times-a-year newsletter features solid coaching skills, plays, diagrams, techniques, drills and hoops management ideas you can put to immediate use. Must reading for basketball coaches at every level.

SEND WINNING HOOPS TO FRIENDS!

This six-times-a-year newsletter also makes a great gift for friends coaching basketball at any level of competition. This newsletter makes a great gift that takes on all aspects of basketball coaching:

- ✔ Defense.
- ✔ Drills.
- ✔ Free throws.
- ✔ Game preparation.
- ✔ Game management.
- ✔ Offense.
- ✔ Personal coaching growth.

- ✔ Coaching philosophies.
- ✔ Player and family relations.
- ✔ Player motivation.
- ✔ Practice management.
- ✔ Hi-tech computer ideas for coaches.
- ✔ Promotion and marketing of a basketball program.

It's a great learning tool that will help you win more games—practically like having another assistant coach sitting on your bench all year long!

Winning Hoops,
P.O. Box 128 • Sparta, MI 49345
Call: 616-887-9008 • Fax: 616-887-2666
www.winninghoops.com

BASELINE OUT-OF-BOUNDS

3-POINT SHOTS

A QUICK LOOK AT THREE OFF INBOUNDS PLAY

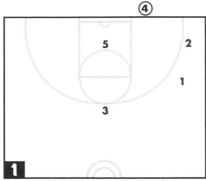

1

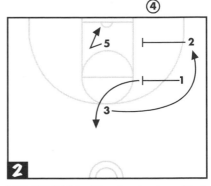

2

DIAGRAM 1: The original set of the play is shown. The inbounder, 4, is tall and a good passer. 3 is the best three-point shooter on the team and lines up at the top of the key. 5 is the best post player and lines up in the middle of the lane. 1 is the point guard and 2 is the other guard. 1 and 2 line up outside the three-point line.

DIAGRAM 2: The play begins with 5 cutting hard to an open gap on the off-side of the basket. At the same time, 2 and 1 screen the wings of the zone, and 3 cuts to the area between 1 and 2, looking for the uncontested three-point shot. 1 cuts out to the top of the key on the inbounds pass to 3 in case 3 does not have the shot. Upon receiving the pass, 1 sets up the offense.

—Kenneth Edwards,
Cox High School,
Virginia Beach, Va.

OUT-OF-BOUNDS PLAY FOR A "THREE"

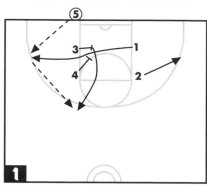

DIAGRAM 1: 4 screens the screener and 1 looks for 3 coming off for the three-point shot.

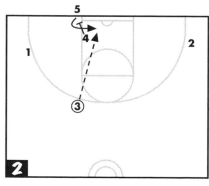

DIAGRAM 2: If you don't get the shot, look for 5 on the post curl off 4's screen.

—Terry Zerr,
Eudora High School,
Eudora, Kan.

THREE-POINT OR TWO-POINT INBOUNDS PLAY

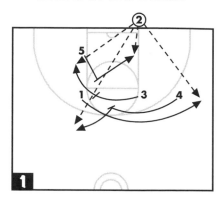

As 2 inbounds, 3 and 4 set a pick for 1. 5 sets a pick for 3, then rolls to the hoop. After setting a pick for 1, 3 rolls to the hoop off 5's pick. 4 is the safety valve. 2 has four options.

Option 1: Pass to 1 beyond the three-point line.

Option 2: Pass to 5 rolling down the lane.

Option 3: Pass to 3 coming off 5's pick.

Option 4: Pass to 4 as the safety. Wherever 2 passes, 2 goes to the opposite side.

—Jon Pye,
Central Missouri State University,
Warrensburg, Mo.

TWO 3-POINT PLAYS FROM BASELINE OUT-OF-BOUNDS

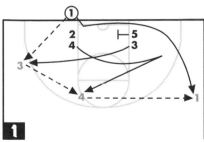

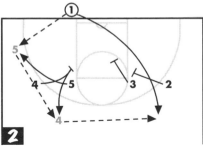

DIAGRAM 1: 3 and 4 loop to opposite sides of the lane. 3 receives the inbounds pass from 1. 4, who has cut to the top of the key, receives the pass from 3. After inbounding the ball to 3, 1 cuts to the opposite side off 5's screen to receive the pass from 4 for a three-point shot.

DIAGRAM 2: 4 sets a pick for 5. 5 comes off the screen to receive the inbounds pass from 1. 5 then passes to 4, who has rolled off the screen to the top of the key. 2 and 3 set a staggered screen. After inbounding to 5, 1 comes off the staggered screen for a pass from 4 and a three-point shot.

—Jon Pye,
Central Missouri State University,
Warrensburg, Mo.

TWO HIGH-EFFICIENCY OUT-OF-BOUNDS PLAYS FOR 3-POINT SHOTS

These plays offer excellent opportunities to set up a three-point shot.

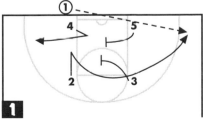

DIAGRAM 1: This play is for use against a man defense. 1 inbounds while 2, 3, 4, and 5 set up in a box formation. 5 and 3 set a double screen for 2 flaring outside the three-point arc for the jumper. The keys here are 1 pass-faking to 4 and 2 setting up the defense by coming to the ball, then cutting off the double screen.

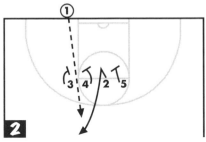

DIAGRAM 2: This play works against a zone defense. As 1 gets ready to inbound the ball, the other players line up on the foul line as shown. 3, 4 and 5 set screens for 2, who steps behind the three-point arc for the jump shot after receiving 1's over-the-top pass. The keys to this play are 1 passing the ball to a spot and 2 faking to the ball, then ducking back out as 4 and 5 close the gap.

—Ron Righter,
University of Southern California,
Los Angeles, Calif.

OUT OF BOUNDS VS. 2-3 ZONE

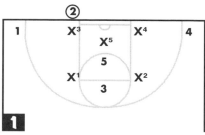

DIAGRAM 1: Basic formation.

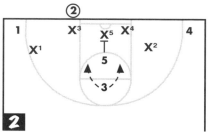

DIAGRAM 2: 2 slaps the ball, then reads the defensive guards. If they play back, inbound to 1 or 4. If the defensive guards slide toward the corners, 5 pins middle defender and 2 inbounds (lob) to 3.

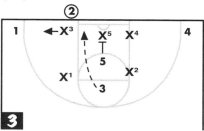

DIAGRAM 3: If defensive forward jumps the corner, 5 pins the middle defender and 3 penetrates the gap.

—Greg Adkins,
Garfield Junior High School,
Hamilton, Ohio

ZONE INBOUNDS PLAY

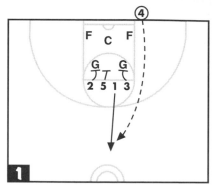

DIAGRAM 1: 4 takes the ball from the official and throws a lob pass to 1 at the top of the key .

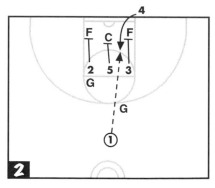

DIAGRAM 2: 2, 5 and 3 set a triple screen. As the ball passes over the top of the triple screen, 2 screens down on a forward, 5 screens down on the center and 3 screens down on the other forward.

4 picks a hole and cuts to the middle of the lane for the entry pass from 1.

—Doug Elledge,
Liberty High School,
Liberty, Ill.

SCREEN-THE-SCREENER OUT-OF-BOUNDS VS. MAN-TO-MAN OR ZONE

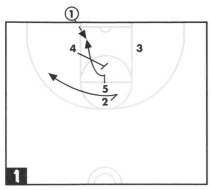

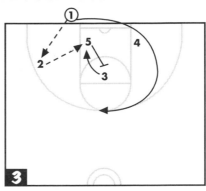

DIAGRAM 1: The alignment (can also be run from a box set). The first option is 5 flashing to the ball off the screen by 4. 2 moves to ball side wing.

—Rick E. Uhrig,
Huntington High School,
Chillicothe, Ohio

INBOUNDS VS. ZONE

This play is used against a defense that zones out-of-bounds.

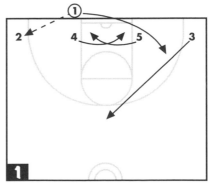

DIAGRAM 2: "Screen-the-Screener" option, 3 back screens for 4 who rolls to the backside of the basket. This is open most of the time. 1 should pass fake to 2 before inbounding to freeze the help.

DIAGRAM 3: The third option is an inbounds pass to 2. 5 back screens for 3, who rolls to the ball side of the basket. 1 enters to the opposite side of the inbounds pass and goes to key area. If the inbounds pass goes to either of the first two options, 2 drifts back to key area as a safety.

DIAGRAMS 1 & 2: Overload the baseline by putting four across. The inbounds pass can go to either wing or to the post player, who is crisscrossing and posting up inside. The passer goes to the opposite side of the inbounds pass. Opposite wing runs to the top of the key. With proper ball movement,

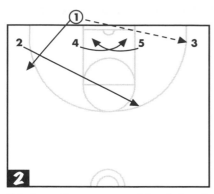

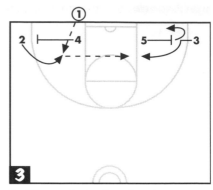

this formation opens up either 1, 2 or 3 for a shot.

DIAGRAM 3: If the team decides to match up against you, send your post players out to screen. 1 passes to 2. 2 looks for 3 cutting off of 5's screen or

5 rolling to the basket after the screen.

—John Ford,
Coatesville High School,
Coatesville, Pa.

QUICK HITTER VS. 2-3 ZONE

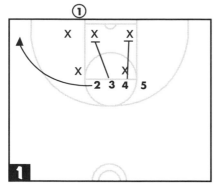

DIAGRAM 1: Put your best three-point shooter at the 2 spot. Use 2 to flatten the defense. 3 and 4 cut to the basket and screen the bottom of the zone.

DIAGRAM 2: 5 hesitates, then moves to the middle of the lane for a lob from 1.

DIAGRAM 3: If 1 can't pass to 5, 4 leaves the lane. 2 and 4 are safety outlets.

—Dale Herl,
Stafford High School,
Stafford, Kan.

LOB VS. MAN OR ZONE

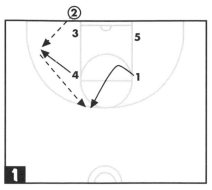

DIAGRAM 1: 4 steps out to get the ball, then passes to 1.

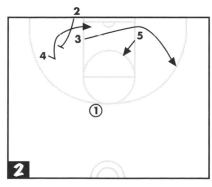

DIAGRAM 2: 3 cuts to the opposite side as 5 flashes to the ball. 2 steps in and sets a back screen for 4.

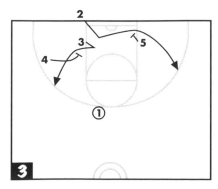

DIAGRAM 3: An option is to have 4 screen down on 3 as 5 screens for 2.

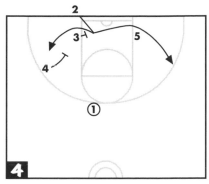

DIAGRAM 4: A third option is to let your shooter choose to use the single screen from 5 or the stagger screen from 3 and 4.

—Lason Perkins,
Cary High School,
Cary, N.C.

OUT-OF BOUNDS PLAY (4 OPTIONS)

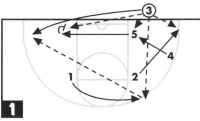

This play may be used against both man-to-man and zone defenses.

Option 1: Pass to 5 sliding in the lane.
Option 2: Pass to 4 slashing to the block.
Option 3: Pass to 2 for the baseline jumper.
Option 4: After inbounding to 1, 1 hits 3 coming off a screen by 5. Timing is important, especially for 2 and 3.

—Bill Agronin,
Niagara University,
Niagara University, N.Y.

INBOUND PLAY VS. 2-3 ZONE

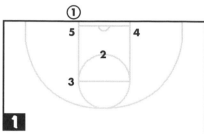

DIAGRAM 1: Your best three-point shooter, 2, stands in the middle of the lane as if to catch a lob. 1 is the inbounder and second-best three-point shooter. 5 and 3 line up along the lane, while 4 is opposite the ball on the block.

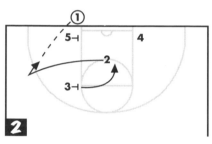

DIAGRAM 2: As soon as the official hands 1 the ball, 2 breaks to the ball side beyond the three-point arc. 3 and 5 will screen the zone defenders. 1 will look hard at 4 before passing to 2, who sets up for a three-point shot. 4 is ready to work the boards. On the shot, 3 joins 5 and 4 on the boards to form a triangle rebounding position.

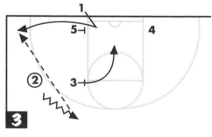

DIAGRAM 3: Should 2 decide not to take a shot, dribble away from the base-

line. 1 steps in bounds toward the basket and breaks off of 5's stationary screen in order to receive a pass from 2 for a three-point shot from the corner. 3, 4 and 5 will form a triangle for rebounding.

—*Al Rabenold,*
Grinnell College,
Grinnell, Iowa

LOB OUT-OF-BOUNDS PLAY VS. ZONE

This lob play from a box set was run several times this past year and resulted in many incredible dunks that were extremely crowd-pleasing. It was the "play of the game" in our state tournament qualifying game. In this play, 4 is the team's best leaper.

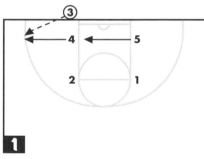

DIAGRAM 1: 4 pops out to the corner and receives the inbounds pass from 3. 5 fills the ball side post position.

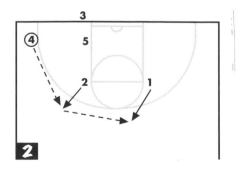

DIAGRAM 2: 4 passes the ball to 2, who passes to 1.
DIAGRAM 3: 5 flashes hard to the middle of the lane, drawing the center of the zone with him. 3 back screens the opposite forward of the zone and 1 alley-oops it to 4 for the dunk.

—Mark Graupe,
Central Middle School,
Devils Lake, N.D.

OUT-OF-BOUNDS VS. ZONE OR MAN

This play works well against any zone or man defense. We have about 90 percent scoring frequency when we run it.

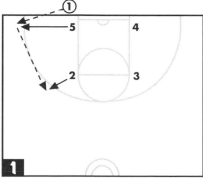

DIAGRAM 1: Out of the box set, player 5 flashes to the corner and takes the inbounds pass from 1. 5 reverses the ball to 2.
DIAGRAM 2: 2 dribbles to improve

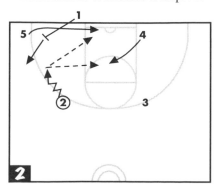

the angle for the lob or flash post. 1 sets a back pick for 5 and 4 flashes to the middle of the lane to the "face" of the middle man of the zone to occupy him. We look to lob to 5 or hit 4 on the flash, if the defense adjusts to the lob.

DIAGRAM 3: 1 steps out as 4 continues to the post to the box set.

—Brian Hocnevar,
Lamar High School,
Lamar, Colo.

INBOUND "SWING" SERIES

These three plays are designed to provide a quick hitter play or to swing the ball to get a shot for the inbound passer (3).

BASIC SET

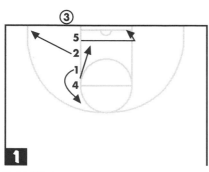

DIAGRAM 1: 5 cuts away and posts up in front of the defender. 2 cuts out to the corner, 1 releases out for safety valve. 4 hesitates and cuts into the open area.

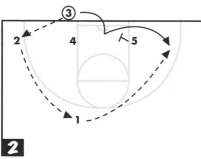

DIAGRAM 2: If no one is open for a quick hitter, 3 inbounds to 2 or 1, steps into the middle of the lane, then pops out on weak side around a screen set by 5.

OPTION TWO

DIAGRAM 3: Against a zone, 5 faces the ball. Against man-to-man, 5 faces 4. If the zone doesn't guard 5 close, 3 and 5 can make eye contact for a quick hitter.

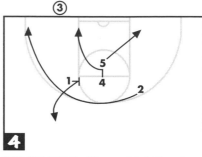

DIAGRAM 4: If no quick hitter, 4 cuts either right or left off of 5. 5 cuts opposite 4. 2 cuts to the strong side corner. 1 sets a pick on the wing defender, then cuts out.

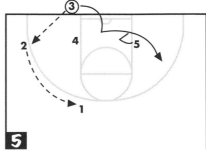

DIAGRAM 5: If no quick hitters are open, continue to swing for 3.

OPTION THREE

DIAGRAM 6: Weak side block player (4) flashes the middle looking for

6

the pass. 1 flashes toward the block.

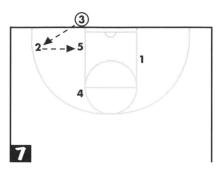

7

DIAGRAM 7: If neither flashers are open, 3 inbounds to 2 in the corner. 2 looks for post up opportunities for 5 first.

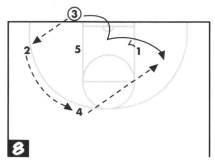

8

DIAGRAM 8: 1 sets a pick for 3 and we work for the swing option to 3.

—Dan Ross,
Fox Chapel High School,
Pittsburgh, Pa.

OUT-OF-BOUNDS STACK

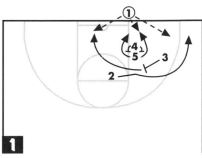

1

1 takes the ball out of bounds. 2 cuts over the screen from 3 to the corner while 3 cuts quick to the other side of the lane. 4 sets a screen for 5 and 5 cuts off 4 on either side looking for the pass from 1.

—Bill Kunze,
Duluth East High School,
Duluth, Minn.

OUT-OF-BOUNDS VS. MAN-TO-MAN

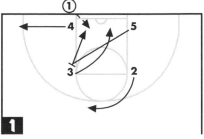

1

Line up in box. 4 breaks to the corner, calling for the ball. 5 diagonally screens for 3, who rolls down the middle looking for a layup. 5 then pins 3's defender and rolls to the hoop for an uncontested layup. 2 is the release who drops back on defense.

—Jim Satalin,
Duquesne University, Pittsburgh, Pa.

INDIAN INBOUNDS PLAY

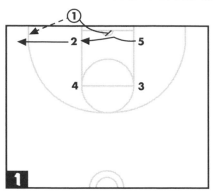

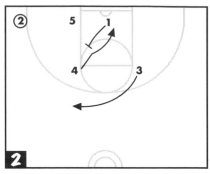

DIAGRAM 1: 2 pops to the corner to receive the inbounds pass. 1 steps in to set a screen for 5 coming across.

DIAGRAM 2: If 5 isn't open, look for 4 on the backside.

—Joe Pitt, Union High School, Union, S.C.

OUT-OF-BOUNDS UNDER THE BASKET

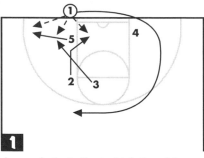

1 pounds the ball, at which time 3 jumps to occupy the defense for a split second. 5 breaks to the sideline as the safety valve. 2 breaks to the basket, as does 3. First option: Hit 2 breaking. Second option: Hit 3 breaking. For a safety valve, hit 5 in the corner. After inbounding the ball, 1 uses 4 as a screen.

—Clem Haskins,
University of Minnesota,
Minneapolis, Minn.

"SCRAMBLE" OUT-OF-BOUNDS PLAY

2 goes to the three-point area, 4 goes to the low block area and 1 sets a screen for 5, who goes to the ball. 1 proceeds out beyond the three-point line as a safety. With slight adjustments, this play can be used against either man-to-man or zone defenses.

—Bill Agronin,
Niagara University,
Niagara University, N.Y.

OUT-OF-BOUNDS SPECIAL PLAY

This out-of-bounds play is designed to attack a man-to-man defense. Players line up in a stack, starting on the block and facing the passer, P (1 is closest to the passer).

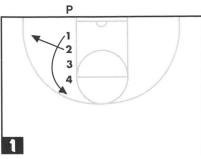

DIAGRAM 1: On the slap of the ball, 1 cuts away from the lane and goes behind. When this player passes 2, 2 pops out, clapping hands and calling for the ball (a good acting job is required here).

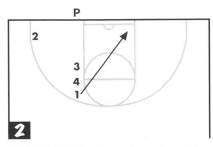

DIAGRAM 2: 1 cuts down the middle from behind 4, looking for the pass and an easy layup.

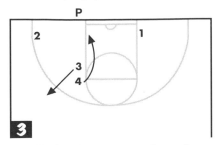

DIAGRAM 3: As soon as 1 cuts the lane, 4 goes to the ball (in case no pass has been made) and 3 pops out to the three-point area on the ball side for two reasons: First, 3 is our last choice for the inbounds pass, second, if 1 receives the ball and makes the basket, 3 can drop back to prevent a fast break. This play must be run at full speed to work.

—Wally Sorensen,
Notre Dame High School,
Batavia, N.Y.

THE "2 PLAY" VS. MAN-TO-MAN

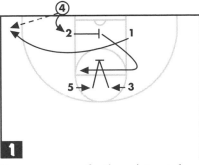

2 screens across for the point guard (1), who pops to the corner. At the same time, 5 and 3 come together and screen down for 2 on the block away from the ball. After 4 inbounds the ball to 1, 4 then posts up on the block. This play leads to an easy jumper for 2 in the lane or a dump into 4 posting up.

—Jerry Mackey,
Oneonta High School,
Oneonta, N.Y.

TRIANGLE VS. MAN INBOUNDS PLAY

We run this inbounds play from the baseline under our own basket. I like this play because it initially develops looking for an inside shot and has the possibility for an outside shot as well if we go all the way to the reversal.

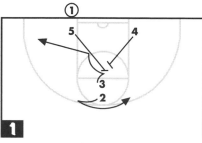

DIAGRAM 1: 2 is at the top of the key and drives left, then drifts back right. 5 goes to set a back pick for 3, who V-cuts off this back pick, looking for the ball on the block. If 3 doesn't get the ball, they drift toward the corner. 4 delays and then goes to set a back pick for 5 in screen-the-screener action.

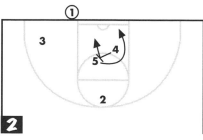

DIAGRAM 2: 4 sets the back pick for 5, then both roll back to the basket.

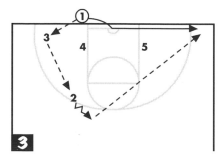

DIAGRAM 3: 4 and 5, aren't open, so the inbounds pass goes to 3, who hits 2 sliding back to the ball side. 2 begins to drive across the key and reverses the ball to 1 in the offside corner.

—Nelson Catalina,
Arkansas State University,
State University, Ark.

INBOUNDS VS. MAN

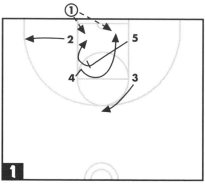

This is an effective play when you have two post players capable of scoring. Our set is from a box set, as is all our man inbound plays, so they are harder to scout.

2 should be a good shooter and should step to the paint before breaking to the corner for a shot. This clears the paint area for 5 to cross screen up to 4. After 5 sets the screen, they roll to the ball.

We find many scoring chances for 4 in a non-switching defense and for 5 in a switching defense. 3 pops high for safety valve purposes as well as for defensive reasons.

—John Ford,
Coatesville High School,
Coatesville, Pa.

INBOUNDS "OPTION" PLAY

This play allows the offense to take advantage of any defensive alignment, and can be used against many zone defenses successfully.

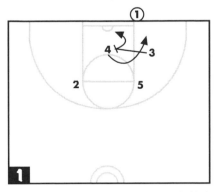

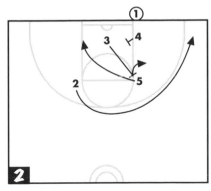

DIAGRAM 1: When 1 slaps the ball, 3 screens for 4, who cuts to the box. 3 seals their defender, curls hard and looks for the ball. 2 and 5 delay a second.

DIAGRAM 2: 3 has the option of setting a back screen for 5 if they cannot seal the defender. 5 cuts to the box off the screen and 3 opens up at the high post. 2 cuts around the key to become the last option.

—John Pretzer,
Bowbells High School,
Bowbells, N.D.

BOX SET OUT-OF-BOUNDS PLAY

In this play, your best scorer (3) takes the ball out.

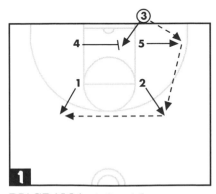

DIAGRAM 1: 1, 2 and 5 pop out to get open. 3 inbounds to 5, who passes to 2, who passes to 1.

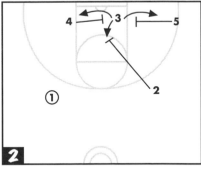

DIAGRAM 2: As 3 steps in to the block, everyone picks for 3, who can go anywhere.

—John Gibson,
University of Tennessee-Chattanooga,
Chattanooga, Tenn.

THREE OUT-OF-BOUNDS PLAYS

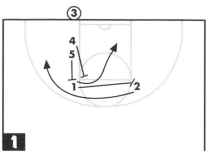

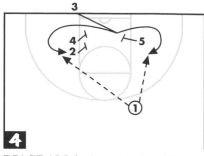

DIAGRAM 1: In this play, 1 sets a screen for 2 while 4 and 5 set a double screen for 2. 5 then goes off 4's screen. 3 can inbound the ball to either 2 or 5.

DIAGRAM 4: 3 can break off the single screen set by 5 or the double screen set by 4 and 2. 1 passes to 3 for the shot.

—Jim Crews,
University of Evansville,
Evansville, Ind.

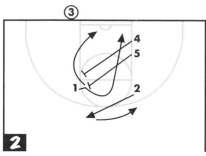

DIAGRAM 2: Here 4 and 5 set a double screen for 1. Then 5 breaks opposite 1 after the screen has been set. 2 rotates back, but must meet the pass, if thrown to them by 3 inbounding the ball.

SCREEN-THE-SCREENER

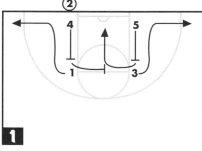

4 and 5 screen for 1 and 3. 1 and 3 go to the block, then move to the corners. 4 screens for 5, who rolls to the basket looking for the score.

—Pat Fischer,
Waynesfield-Goshen Schools,
St. Mary's, Ohio

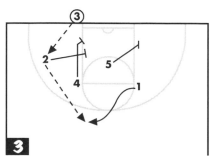

DIAGRAM 3: In this situation 3 passes to 2, who passes to 1 after 1 has rotated to the ball side. 5 sets a screen and 2 and 4 set a double screen.

OUT-OF-BOUNDS SPECIAL PLAY

This out-of-bounds play is designed to attack man-to-man defenses. It has worked so well for us that we once scored five times in one game on this play.

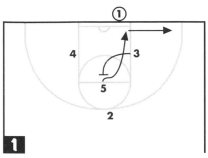

DIAGRAM 1: As 1 slaps the ball, 3 picks for 5, who rolls to the block looking for the ball. If 5 doesn't receive it, 5 goes baseline.

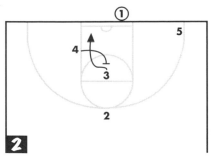

DIAGRAM 2 (Best option): 4 delays, then picks 3's defender in the paint. 3 rolls to the block looking for the ball (and is usually wide open).

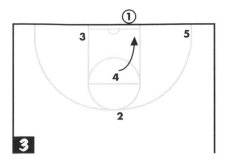

DIAGRAM 3: After 4 picks, they pivot and roll hard to get the ball on the block. If all fails, 2 finds a gap and gets the ball. We've never had to pass to 2 in five years of running this play.

—Cayll Smith,
Riverview High School,
Sarasota, Fla.

DIAGONAL

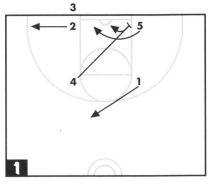

2 breaks to the corner.
1 is a safety.
4 screens diagonally for 5.
5 rolls off of 4's screen to the ball.
4 pivots to the basket.
3 passes to 5 or 4.

—Bud Hazelwood,
Hampton High School,
Hampton, Tenn.

UNDER THE BASKET INBOUNDS PLAY

This play works against man or zone defenses. We call it "Boxer".

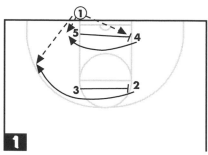

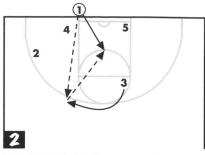

DIAGRAM 1: 5 and 3 screen across at the same time. 1 looks to pass the ball to 5, who reverse pivots under the basket for a right-handed layup. The next option is to look for 4 coming to the ball for a left-handed layup, and 2 is the third option for a jump shot on the left side of the lane.

DIAGRAM 2: These are our last options. 1 passes to safety outlet 3. After looking to 2 in the corner, 3 passes back to 1, who has stepped into the middle of the lane. 1 sometimes gets an easy basket or draws a foul.

—Jerry Coulter,
Powder River County High School,
Broadus, Mont.

POINT CURL

We've averaged three shots a game (two makes) off this play. Most defenses think 1 is usually the safety and that's what makes this play successful.

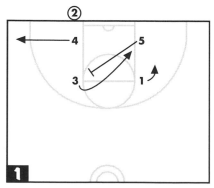

DIAGRAM 1: 4 pops to the corner. 5 sets a diagonal screen for 3 who goes to the opposite block. 1 starts cut away.

DIAGRAM 2: 5 then turns and sets a screen for 1. 1 curls outside of lane for a 10-foot jumper. 5 drops out as safety. 3 posts for rebound.

—Marty Cline,
North Hopkins High School,
Madisonville, Ky.

TAKE 2—A CAN'T MISS INBOUNDS PLAY

I have used these inbounds plays for more than 20 years and have enjoyed continual and tremendous success with them!

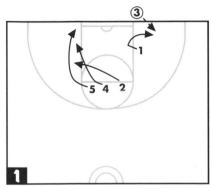

DIAGRAM 1: In this basic setup, 3 should be your best shooter and passer and 1 should be your point guard. On the break, 1 jab steps and breaks out on the baseline. 5, 4 and 2 set up a triple screen on the opposite side of the lane.

DIAGRAM 2: 3 passes to 1, then jab steers toward 1 and goes to the opposite side of the triple screen. 1 then passes over the triple screen to 3.

After running this option a few times, you have set up the following two options.

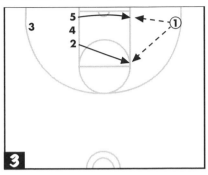

DIAGRAM 3: 1 has already received the ball and 3 is opposite the screen. 2 and 5 hold the screen briefly and allow the defense to fight through. Then they break to the ball at the high and low post.

DIAGRAM 4: Using the same inbounds pass and the same moves for 4 and 5, 2 breaks out to the ball side and receives the pass from 1. 3 uses a jab-step fake to the opposite screen and 1 picks the low post defender. 3 uses the back pick and receives the ball from 2 for a baseline shot.

—Bill Laurich,
Marquette High School,
Marquette, Mich.

INBOUNDS PLAY

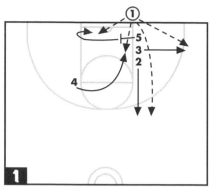

DIAGRAM 1: Against a zone defense, 5 screens nearest defender to get inside position on the weak side block. 3 cuts to the ball side corner. 2 backs up and acts as a safety release outside the three-point line. 4, your best leaper, circles and goes down the lane toward the ball.

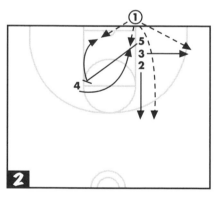

DIAGRAM 2: Against a man-to-man defense, the cuts are the same except for 5, who sets a diagonal back screen for 4, then rolls down to the weak side box. 4 must wait for the screen to get open.

—Teresa C. Bentley,
Jenkins High School,
Jenkins, Ky.

BASELINE OUT-OF-BOUNDS

This out-of-bounds play is designed to get a jump shot for the inbounder or an easy basket off a weak side flex cut. It works against man or zone defenses.

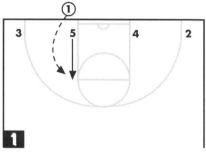

DIAGRAM 1: When 1 gets the ball, 5 flashes up the lane to the elbow (If the defense is unprepared as 1 receives the ball from the official, a lob underneath may be available.)

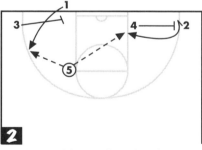

DIAGRAM 2: As 5 catches the pass, 4 steps out to set a screen for 2. 2 flex cuts off 4's screen ready to receive a pass. Simultaneously 3 finds the inbounder's defender and sets a down screen, then seals. 5 passes to open player. If nobody is open, 1 sprints to 5 for short pass or hand-off.

—Raymond Townsend,
Menlo College,
San Jose, Calif.

FLEX INBOUNDS VS. MAN

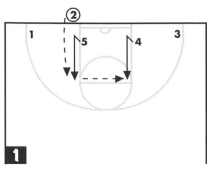

DIAGRAM 1: Set up with 4 players across the baseline. 5 V-cuts up to the elbow for the pass from 2.

If 5's defender is overplaying, then 5 should flash back to the basket. After 5 catches ball, 4 cuts to the opposite elbow. If 4's defender overplays, 4 should attack the back door.

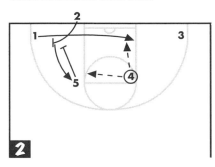

DIAGRAM 2: After 4 catches the ball, 1 makes a flex-cut off 2's pick coming inbound after the initial pass. 5 down screens for 2. 4 looks for 1, then to 2.

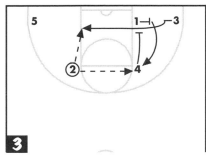

DIAGRAM 3: If 4 passes to 2, 3 makes a flex cut off 1's screen. The play continues until the proper shot presents itself. *Note:* If 5 has trouble getting open initially, 5 can pick for 1. 1 goes to the elbow for the pass from 2 and 5 will flex-cut off 2's screen.

—Donnie Hand,
Cleburne County High School,
Hefline, Ala.

BASELINE OUT-OF-BOUNDS PLAY

This is a counter to the traditional screen-the-screener action.

DIAGRAM 1: 1 clears out quickly.

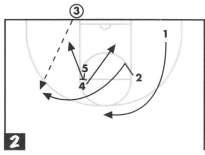

DIAGRAM 2: Entry pass goes from 3 to 2, if the lob pass to 4 is not open.

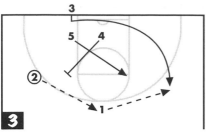

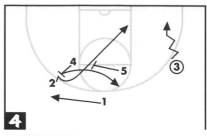

DIAGRAM 3: Swing ball around from 2 to 1 to 3. 5 and 4 cross with 4 setting a screen for 2.

DIAGRAM 4: 3 can go one-on-one with defender. 2 uses 4's screen. Then 4 comes off 5's screen.

—Craig Jonas, Coach's Edge, Lawrence, Kan.

INBOUNDS PLAY

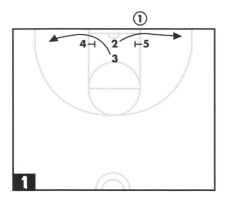

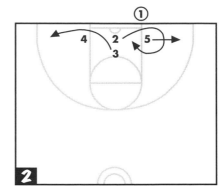

DIAGRAM 1: 5, the best post player on the team, screens for 2, the best shooter, who goes for a possible three-pointer. 4 screens for 3. 4 then seals. 4 and 5 look for lobs. This is especially effective against the 2-3 zone.

DIAGRAM 2: 2 or 3 can curl if the defense begins to cheat. If this happens, 5 should step to the short corner.

DIAGRAM 3: 2 or 3 release. 5 and 4 step out to back screen.

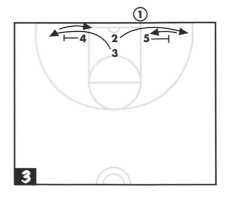

—Kent Christian, Greenbush Middle River High School, Greenbush, Minn.

EFFECTIVE INBOUNDS PLAY

These are two simple baseline inbounds plays—one against a man-to-man defense and the other against a zone defense.

Both plays have given us many good shot opportunities.

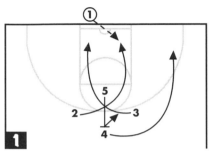

DIAGRAM 1: In this set, 3 and 2 scissor off 5. 5 can screen for 4, who fades to the corner after 2 and 3 scissor. 5 can then roll back after the screen. 1 can hit 2 or 3.

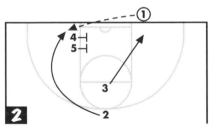

DIAGRAM 2: Against a zone defense, 3 dives to 1 while calling for the ball. 2 cuts behind the double screen set by 4 and 5. 2 receives a pass for the jumper. 5 may release to the ball if the defense gets lazy.

Note: 1's pass will be from a tough angle, so the player must be stationary. If the double stack is on the opposite side of the lane, the ideal situation would be for a left-handed player to inbound the ball.

—Bob Sonday,
Monsignor Donovan High School,
Toms River, N.J.

BOX VS. MAN

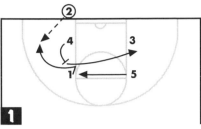

DIAGRAM 1: 4 steps up and screens for 1. 1 cuts off 4's screen and receives the ball. 4 moves across the lane after screening as 5 comes across the top of the lane.

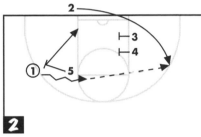

DIAGRAM 2: 5 steps out and sets a ball screen for 1. 1 uses the screen and drives to the middle. 5 rolls to the basket. 3 and 4 set a staggered double screen for 2.

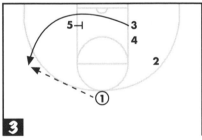

DIAGRAM 3: If 2 is not open, 3 cuts to the opposite side and uses 5's screen to get open for the shot.

—Lason Perkins,
Cary High School,
Cary, N.C.

STACK

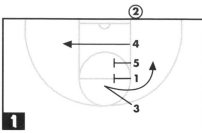

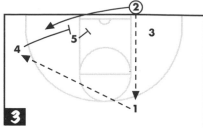

DIAGRAM 1: 4 sprints to the corner. 3 steps hard toward the lane. 1 and 5 set a double screen. 3 curls off the double screen.

DIAGRAM 3: If players 3 and 5 are covered, 2 passes to 1 and cuts off the double screen set by 5 and 4 for the open jump shot.

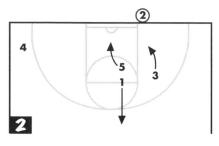

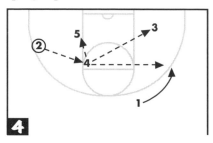

DIAGRAM 2: 5 dives to the basket on a switch. 1 goes to the top of the key for the outlet.

DIAGRAM 4: 4 curls up the lane looking for a pass from 2, then passes to 5, 3 or 1.

—Steve Smith, Oak Hill Academy, Mouth of Wilson, Va.

BASELINE OUT-OF-BOUNDS PLAY

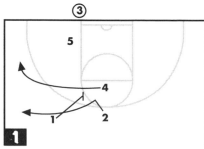

DIAGRAM 1: 5 demands the ball while 4 sprints to an opening or gap against the zone.

DIAGRAM 2: Swing the ball quickly from 4 to 2. 3 steps inbounds immediately.

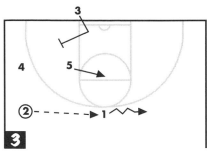

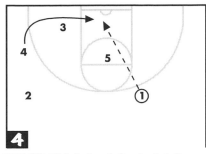

DIAGRAM 3: As the ball is swung from 2 to 1, 5 continues to be active and 3 sets a back screen on the last defender. 1 can dribble to improve the passing angle.

DIAGRAM 4: Look for the lob from 1 to 4 (can disguise as a shot).

—Craig Jonas, Coach's Edge, Lawrence, Kan.

CLIPPER

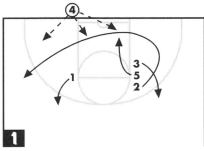

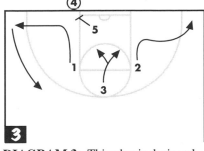

DIAGRAM 1: This out-of-bounds play is for 2 going around 5 and 3. 5 dives to the basket for a second option. 1 fades for a safety outlet.

DIAGRAM 3: This play is designed for 3 to delay and read the defensive reaction to 5, 1 and 2. At times 5 will shake open for an easy basket. 1 and 2 should be open as secondary options.

—Rich Ward, University of Maine at Machias, Machias, Maine

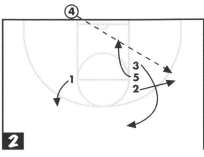

DIAGRAM 2: If 2's defender plays in the paint, 2 reads and steps back for three-pointer using 5 and 3 as screens.

UNDERNEATH VS. MAN-TO-MAN

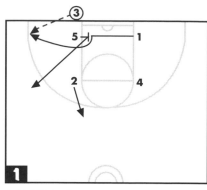

DIAGRAM 1: 5 must set a screen for 1 who must get open in the corner.

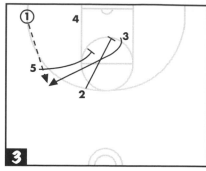

DIAGRAM 3: As 4 is posting, 5 and 2 set a double staggered screen for 3 (5 needs to be the second screen).

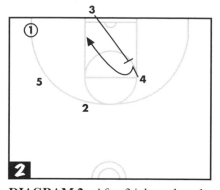

DIAGRAM 2: After 3 inbounds to 1, 3 sets a diagonal screen for 4, who can go to either side around the screen.

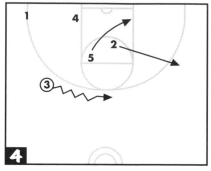

DIAGRAM 4: After 1 passes to 3, 5 dives to the block and 2 goes to the wing for a 3-out, 2-in set.

—Ricky Norris, Oak Ridge High School, Oak Ridge, Tenn.

BASELINE OUT-OF-BOUNDS

PLAY ONE

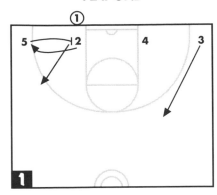

DIAGRAM 1: 5 screens for 2, then pops to the wing. 1 can pass to 2 for the open shot or lob to 5. 3 releases for a safety valve.

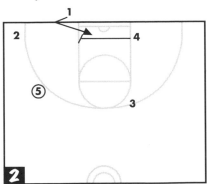

DIAGRAM 2: If 1 passes to 5, 1 V-cuts towards 2 and back into the lane and receives a screen from 4.

PLAY TWO

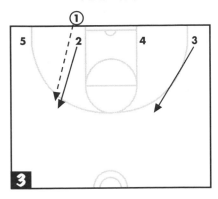

DIAGRAM 3: 2 and 3 pop to the wing. 1 passes to 2.

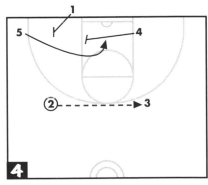

DIAGRAM 4: 1 and 4 screen for 5 as 2 reverse passes to 3. 3 looks to pass to 5 rolling to the basket.

—Tim Foor,
Shikellamy High School,
Sunbury, Pa.

SAVE BIG
with the Winning Hoops Off-Season Package!

Everything you need to build your off-season program.

All this for $39 + S/H

Basketball Forms Book – a book of 93 forms. Foreword written by Shaka Smart! Organize. Save time. Improve record keeping. Train assistants. Make decisions. Win more games.
Original Price: **$34.95**

Perfect Practice Drills – 160 pages loaded with more than 70 of the most creative and time-tested drills from the top high school and college coaches across the nation.
Original Price: **$19.95**

Success In The Off-Season – a 16-page Special Coaching Report helping teams develop a superior off-season program, including an off-season calendar checklist, summer-progress chart and open-gym drills.
Original Price: **$9.95**

Pumping Up Your Off-Season Workouts – a unique 16-page report offering a variety of strength and conditioning workouts designed to boost your players' physical stamina and coordination.
Original Price: **$9.95**

That's a savings of **50%**

Impact your team's training program and season preparation with this great package deal from Winning Hoops. Two books, two reports – **a value of $74.80** – all for **$39** when you order today!

Priority Code: HW1112BBST

Call 616-887-9008, ext. 115.
Ask for the off-season package.

Chapter 3

QUICK HITTERS

QUICK HITTER OUT OF A 1-4 SET

The 1-4 offensive set offers a multitude of scoring opportunities. We utilize a quick-hitting play to get the ball into the hands of one of our better offensive players. Many time8s we run this play after our initial man-to-man offense has broken down and we only have 10 seconds or less on the shot clock.

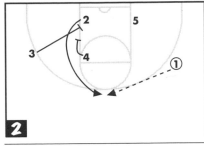

—Bill Agronin,
Niagara University,
Niagara University, N.Y

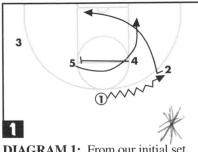

DIAGRAM 1: From our initial set, the point guard is free to choose either side to initiate the play. Our first option is to get the ball to 5 who is rolling low after coming off 4's screen. This is an effective quick-hitting play especially if 5 is a strong post player.

DIAGRAM 2: The second option is to get the ball to 2 who is coming off staggered screens from 3 and 4. This option should allow a three-point shot opportunity.

The key to the success of this play is the timing. 3 must time their screen so that it coincides with 5 rolling low. This will give the defense multiple options to defend.

QUICK SHOT OFFENSE

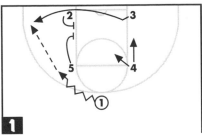

1 dribbles to the wing to set up the pass to 3. 3 cuts off the double screen set up by 5 and 2. 1 passes to 3. Pick away if no shot occurs.

—Van Chancellor,
University of Mississippi,
Oxford, Miss.

QUICK HITTER VS. MAN-TO-MAN

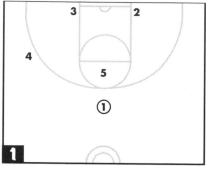

DIAGRAM 1: In this setup, start with your best post player (5) in the middle of the free-throw lane, obviously outside the lane area. Position 2 on the right block and 3 on the left block.

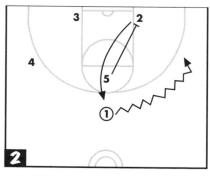

DIAGRAM 2: Once the play is initiated by either a hand signal or a verbal cue, 5 will down screen for 2 while the point guard dribbles to the right wing to create a passing angle to 5. 1's first option is to feed the ball to 5 in the post.

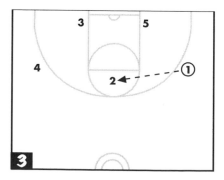

DIAGRAM 3: The second option is to look for 2 coming up to the free-throw line after receiving the screen from 5. If the defense switches, there is an excellent chance that this could create a mismatch (big-on-small) and a subsequent scoring opportunity. If the defense does not switch, 5 should be able to seal their defender on the block.

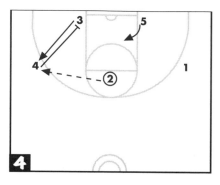

DIAGRAM 4: If the ball is thrown to 2, 2 has the first option of a jump shot, followed by ball reversal to 3, who has come off a weak side exchange screen from 4.

DIAGRAM 5: 3 can either look for a shot, look to 4 in the post or even look for 5 stepping into the lane for a scoring opportunity.

—Mike Mondello,
University of Florida,
Gainesville, Fla.

QUICK SCORE VS. AGGRESSIVE MAN-TO-MAN

DIAGRAM 1: 1 dribbles and passes to the wing. 5 sets a back screen for 1. 3 looks for 1.

DIAGRAM 2: As 1 comes off the back screen, 4 steps up to back screen for 5. 3 looks for 5 as a second option.

DIAGRAM 3: If neither option is open, 3 will reverse the ball to the top to 4. 4 should have an open three-point shot or reverse the ball to 2, who looks to 1 posting up.

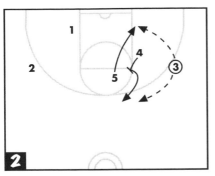

—Ken Phillips,
North Surry High School,
Mt. Airy, N.C.

1—4 set

QUICK HITTER FOR THREE

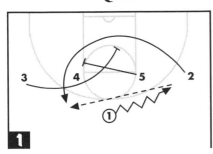

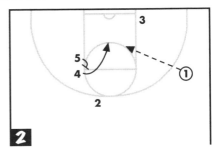

DIAGRAM 1: 1 dribbles to the wing area. 4 and 5 set a double screen for 3, who rolls off the screen to the basket. At the same time 2 loops around the double screen to the top of the key for a three-point shot.

DIAGRAM 2: If 2 does not get a pass, 5 sets a back screen for 4 rolling to the basket for the lob pass.

—Bill Agronin, Niagara University,
Niagara University, N.Y.

QUICK HITTER OUT OF BOX SET

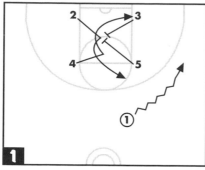

DIAGRAM 1: Point guard is below the foul line extended, but not too far over the midpoint. Patience is a key. 3 and 5 set a double screen.

4 and 2 shuffle cut off the double screen with 2 curling out at the top. Look for 4 on the box.

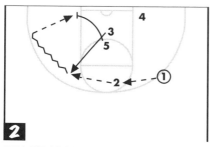

DIAGRAM 2: 3 clears out opposite the double screen and 5 goes to the opposite box.

DIAGRAM 3: This represents an option. Swing the ball left to 3. 3 and 5 then play a two-player game.

DIAGRAM 4: Another option off the play. 3 still has possession of the ball and calls out 5 for the pick and roll. Automatic down screen on the opposite side. 1 is the safety.

—Nate Webber,
McCorristin Catholic High School,
Trenton, N.J.

QUICK HITTER

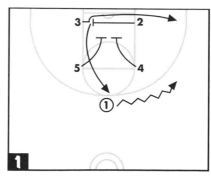

DIAGRAM 1: 1 dribbles to the wing. 2 screens 3, who pops to the corner. 4 and 5 double screen for 2, who pops to the top of the key for a shot.

—Pat Fischer,
Waynesfield-Goshen School,
St. Mary's, Ohio

QUICK HITTER OUT OF A STACK

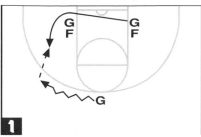

1

DIAGRAM 1: Initially, look for a quick hit option for one of the guards coming off the double screen.

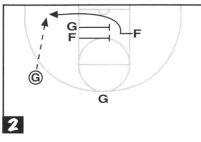

DIAGRAM 2: If there is no shooting option, the guard and forward screen across the lane for the opposite forward.

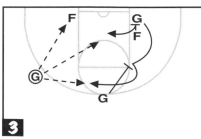

DIAGRAM 3: If the forward is not open, the forward and guard set screens for the player at the bottom of the stack. It is very important that players step back after they screen.

—Nate Webber,
McCorristin Catholic High School,
Trenton, N.J.

QUICK HITTER

This quick hitter is run out of a box set. Always start in the same set. The play can be run against a man-to-man or zone defenses. It has multiple options and provides inside-outside balance.

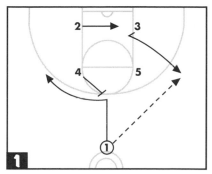

DIAGRAM 1: Enter to either wing. 1 uses a flare screen after passing to 3, who V-cuts to get open on the wing. 2 cuts to ball side block.

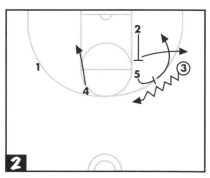

DIAGRAM 2: 3 uses 5's ball screen and moves toward the top of the key. 4 dives and ducks in. 2 sets a back screen for the ball-screener 5, who curls toward the ball side block. 2 pops out for the three-point shot. 3 can hit 5 cutting toward the basket or 2 moving toward the corner for the three-pointer.

—Craig Jonas,
The Coach's Edge,
Lawrence, Kan.

A QUICK HITTER OUT OF A 1-4 SET

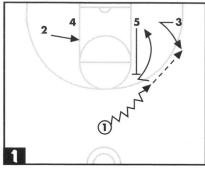

DIAGRAM 1: 1 dribbles up to the right or left of center. 4 or 5 (5 in this case) flashes up to the foul line area. 1 passes the ball to 3 coming out, then cuts off 5's screen.

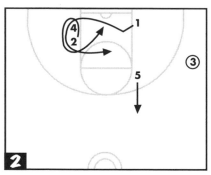

DIAGRAM 2: At the same time, 2 and 4 set a double screen on the left block. 1 curls around the double screen and back into the lane. After 1 goes by, 2 curls around 4 and into the lane. 3 hits either 1 or 2 in the lane.

DIAGRAM 3 : 1 dribbles at 3, who then goes around the double screen being set by 2 and 4.

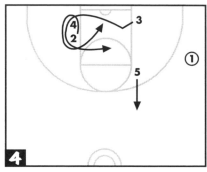

DIAGRAM 4: 2 follows 3 into the lane. 1 hits either 3 or 2 in the lane.

—Bill Agronin,
Niagara University,
Niagara University, N.Y.

ZONE STACK:
A QUICK HITTER AGAINST A 2-3 OR 1-2-2- ZONE

For this play to work well, 2 must be a good three-point shooter and a good penetrator.

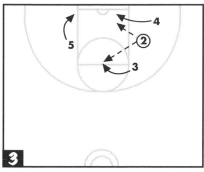

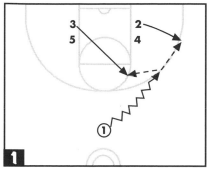

DIAGRAM 1: When 1 dribbles to the wing, both 2 and 3 make their respective cuts. If 1 can get the ball to 3, 3 can either shoot or pass to 4 or 5 for a shot and the play is over. If 1 passes the ball to 2 and the defense does not come out, 2 can take the open three-pointer.

DIAGRAM 3: The two screeners then roll—4 to the basket and 3 to the foul line. The defense will be forced to bring someone from the weak side to stop the ball, leaving 4, 5 or 3 open.

—Kevin Sivils,
Runnels High School,
Rouge, La.

DIAGRAM 2: If the defense goes out to cover 2, then 4 steps out and sets a screen so 2 can drive the middle. 3 sets a screen on the high defender and 2 drives the gap created.

QUICK HITTER VS. MAN-TO-MAN

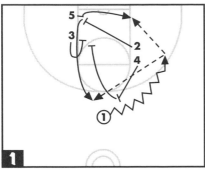

DIAGRAM 1: From the high-low stacks, 1 dribbles off a ball screen set by 4. 2 screens across for 5, who cuts into the low post. 1 looks for 5, or for 2 coming off a double screen set by 4 and 3.

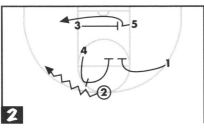

DIAGRAM 2: If 1 passes to 2, 2 can shoot or dribble over to the wing area off 4's screen. When 2 gets to the wing, 3 screens across for 5. 4 and 1 move into the lane and set a double screen.

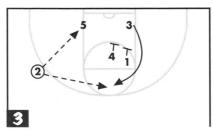

DIAGRAM 3: 2 can pass to 5 or to 3 coming off the double screen.

—Lason Perkins,
Cary High School, Cary, N.C.

QUICK SCORE VS. AGGRESSIVE MAN-TO-MAN DEFENSE

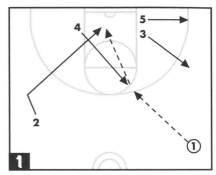

DIAGRAM 1: 1 and 2 are spread out wide. 3 flashes to the wing area and 5 steps out to the corner. As 1 makes a hard spin dribble move, 4 flashes hard to the foul line toward 1 for the pass. 2 makes a hard back door cut to the basket and gets a blind bounce pass from 4. If 2 beats their defender they have an uncontested layup.

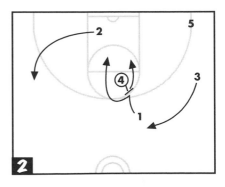

DIAGRAM 2: If 4 cannot pass to 2, then 2 flares away from the ball. 1 then runs their defender off 4 in a give and go action and 3 rotates to the spot 1 vacated for the defense.

—Al Stumpf,
Voorhees High School,
Glen Gardner, N.J.

Chapter 4

PLAYS VS. ZONES

PICK AND ROLL VS. 2-3 ZONE

DIAGRAM 1: Start in a 2-1-2 set.

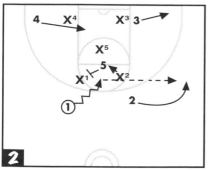

DIAGRAM 2: 5 steps out and screens for 1 while 2 moves into shooting position. X2 should be forced to help on 1, leaving 2 open for the shot at the wing.

DIAGRAM 3: If X3 steps out to take the shooter, 2 looks for 3 in the short corner. 3 looks to score or drive and dish.

DIAGRAM 4: If X5 moves to cover the short corner, 2 can hit 5 after the screen.

—Brent Lemond,
Vanguard High School,
Ocala, Fla.

HIGH PERCENTAGE SHOT VS. ZONE DEFENSE

This play works well for us when we need a high percentage shot vs. a zone defense. It starts with a double low post and can be run to either side.

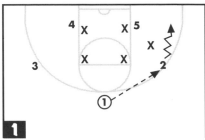

DIAGRAM 1: 1 enters to 2, who takes a couple of dribbles to the baseline to force the zone to shift. 3 sets up high on the opposite wing.

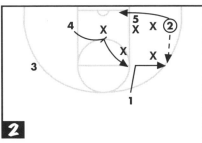

DIAGRAM 2: 2 returns the ball to 1 and immediately cuts across the baseline. As soon as 1 has the ball, 4 flashes into the lane, working hard for the ball. After pausing in the lane to occupy the back side zone defender, 4 continues to the high post.

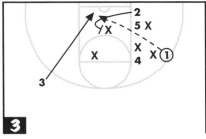

DIAGRAM 3: 2 sets a back pick on the back side zone player. 3 then cuts to the block behind 2's screen for a lob pass from 1 and an easy layup.

Coaching Points: The timing of 4's cut to the high post, 2's back pick and 3's cut to the block is critical to prevent defensive recognition or a three-second violation. Both posts must actively work for position during the play. Finally, 1 must not give away the lob pass with their eyes. 1 should look into the low post before passing.

—Peter C. Moe,
Washburn High School,
Washburn, N.D.

LOB VS. ZONE

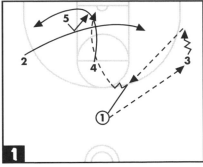

1 passes to 3, who takes one or two dribbles toward the baseline and back out one dribble. With the pass back to 1, 4 cuts below 5 and 2 cuts across the lane, but close to 5. 1 takes one or two dribbles and puts a pass up in the air for 5. If the players are young, just complete the pass. We like to throw the pass off the front of the rim and let 5 go get it. This is a special play and should be used only at special times or to start the second half, etc.

—Jim Rosborough,
Northern Illinois University,
DeKalb, Ill.

TRIPLE VS. 2-3 AND 3-2 ZONES

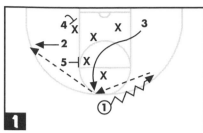

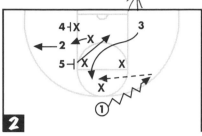

DIAGRAM 1: Against a 2-3 zone, 1 dribbles to the right as 3 replaces on top. As 5 screens in the guard and 4 screens in the forward, 2 pops out. 1 passes to 3, who hits 2.

DIAGRAM 2: Against a 3-2 zone, we run the same set, but if 2's defender jumps out, 3 ball fakes to 2 and 5 steps into the lane.

—Jim O'Brien, Boston College, Chestnut Hill, Mass.

INBOUND VS. 2-3 ZONE

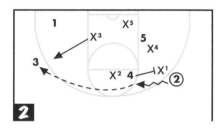

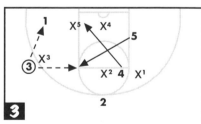

DIAGRAM 1: This play is designed to create a mismatch for your perimeter player who has the ability to finish near the basket. Begin in a 1-3-1 look with a pass to 2 at the wing. 1 moves to the corner on the weak side. 2 must catch the ball above the free-throw line. X1 will move out to guard 2. 3 moves into position below the free-throw line.

DIAGRAM 2: 2 goes hard off the ball screen by 4. 2 passes to 3. 2 can pass to 1 if X3 cheats.

DIAGRAM 3: 3 has three options: hit 1 isolated against X5 in the short corner, pass to 4 diving to the block if X5 cheats to cover 1, or pass to 5 in the mid-post for a jump shot or dump down to 4.

Adjustments: You can have 2 or 3 slide down to the short corner and 1 slide to the wing on the initial pass.

—Ricky Norris,
Oak Ridge High School,
Oak Ridge, Tenn.

OVERLOAD VS. ZONE OFFENSE

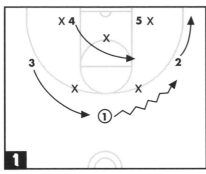

DIAGRAM 1: 1 dribbles to either side, pushing the perimeter player to the corner. The opposite perimeter player replaces 1. 4 flashes high to the opposite elbow.

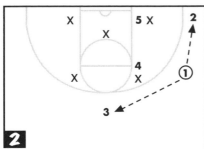

DIAGRAM 2: 1 can pass to 2 or 3.

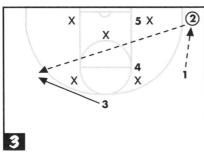

DIAGRAM 3: If 1 passes to 2, 3 stretches the defense to receive the skip pass.

DIAGRAM 4: If 2 returns the pass to 1, 2 runs the baseline off screens by 5 and 4. 4 slashes through the lane to the low block to set up a screen for 2. 1 reverses the ball to 3.

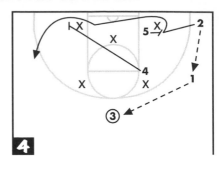

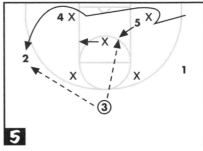

DIAGRAM 5: As soon as 2 comes off 5's screen. 5 flashes toward the ball. 3 can pass to either 5 or 2 coming off the double screen.

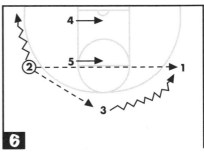

DIAGRAM 6: 2 can dribble into the corner, skip pass to 1 or choose a shorter pass to 3. This starts the motion. 3 becomes the primary ball handler and begins motion by pushing the guard into the corner with the dribble.

*—Nate Webber,
McCorristin Catholic High School,
Trenton, N.J.*

Chapter 5

PLAYS VS. MAN-TO-MAN

3-POINT SHOTS

THREE-POINT SHOT PLAY

DIAGRAM 1: 5 sets up at the top of the key. 1 passes to 5 and sets a screen for 2.

DIAGRAM 2: 2 cuts off the screen by 1. 5 hands off to 2 for the three-pointer, then pivots to cut off the defender.

DIAGRAM 3: On a miss, 2 spots up on the right wing and 1 spots up on the left wing. 5 goes to the glass. Look for a kick-out to the left or right.

—Rich Zvosec,
University of North Florida,
Jacksonville, Fla.

A THREE-POINT PLAY WITH MULTIPLE OPTIONS

This play gives several different three-point shot options.

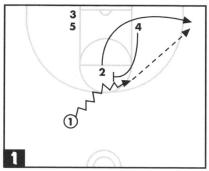

DIAGRAM 1: 2 cuts through the lane and rubs off 4, then sets up behind the three-point line. 4 sets a high post screen for 1, who dribbles off looking to draw 2's defender, allowing 1 to pass to 2 for a three-pointer. After screening on the ball, 4 can roll to the basket or step back for a shot—perhaps a three-pointer.

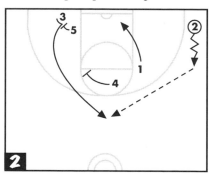

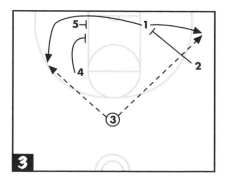

DIAGRAM 2: If 2 doesn't have the shot, 2 can dribble out and look for 3 coming out to the three-point line off a staggered double screen by 5 and 4. 1 cuts slowly to the block and stays.

DIAGRAM 3: If 3 doesn't have the shot, 3 looks to hit 1 coming off either a double screen by 4 and 5 or a screen by 2.

—*Marty Gillespie,*
Bradley University,
Peoria, Ill.

SPECIAL THREE-POINT PLAY

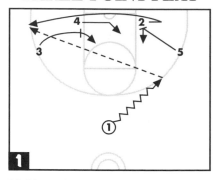

1 initiates the play by dribbling to the wing. At this time, 2 (your best shooter) influences their defender as if they're accepting 5's down screen. 2 then reverses out of the back side off two backward picks by 4 and 3. 2's defender will not chase away (following good defensive principles), leaving 2 open on the cross-court pass from 1.

—*Mack McCarthy,*
University of Tennessee-Chattanooga,
Chattanooga, Tenn.

A QUICK "3" (WITH OPTION)

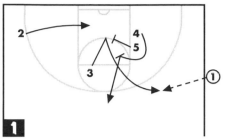

1

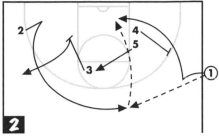

2

DIAGRAM 1: 4 and 5 set a screen for 3, 1 passes the ball to 3 for a quick three-point shot. After setting the screen 4 rolls out for a safety release.

OPTION

DIAGRAM 2: 3 sets a down screen for 2 and rolls out. 1 inbounds the ball to 2.

5 flashes the high post, 4 sets a back screen for 1. 2 can either shoot the three-pointer or lob to 1 cutting to the basket.

—Vinod Vachani,
Welham Girls' High School,
Dehar Dun, India

A QUICK "3"

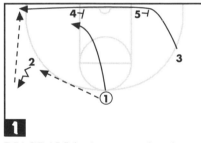

1

2

DIAGRAM 1: 1 passes to 2 and goes to set a double screen with 4. 2 dribbles out, then turns to pass to 3 coming off a screen by 5 and the double screen.
DIAGRAM 2: This play can also be used to get the ball to the post. 4 screens across for 5 and 1 breaks across to the opposite wing. 3 can take

the three-pointer, hit 5 coming across or swing the ball around to 2 to 1 for the weak side shot.

—Tammy Hedspeth,
St. Gertrude High School,
Richmond, Va.

THREE-POINT SHOT FOR YOUR BEST SHOOTER

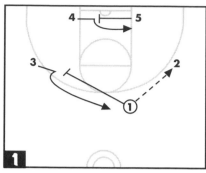

DIAGRAM 1: 1 passes to the wing and screens away. The post to the ball side (5 in diagram) screens across to free 4. 4 is only a decoy.

DIAGRAM 2: 2 reverses the ball to 3. 5, 4 and 2 set a triple screen for 1 for the three-pointer.

—Jimmy Brown, Georgia Southern, Statesboro, Ga.

WEAVE FOR A THREE-POINTER

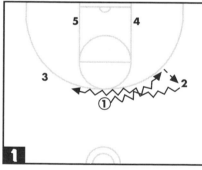

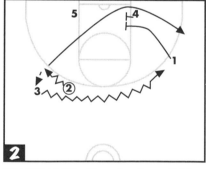

In this situation, the offense needs a quick hitter for a three-pointer. This play works especially well against teams that switch on the dribble handoff.

DIAGRAM 1: 1 executes a dribble handoff to 2 and fills 2's position on the wing. 2 immediately looks for the shot off the temporary screen by 1 on the handoff.

DIAGRAM 2: If no shot is available, 2 executes a dribble handoff with 3, who immediately looks for the shot off the temporary screen by 2. At the same time, 2 is cutting off a double screen set by 4 and 1 on the off-side block. 3 should dribble across the top and look for 2 coming off the screen.

—Kenneth Edwards, Cox High School, Virginia Beach, Va.

THREE-POINT OPTION OFF THE UCLA HIGH POST

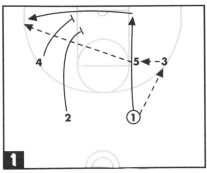

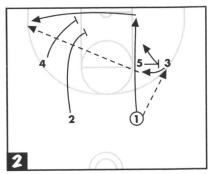

DIAGRAM 1: 1 passes to 3 and cuts off 5's pick. On 3's pass to 5, 4 and 2 set a double screen on the block. 1 goes off this double screen, gets a skip pass from 5 and takes the shot.

DIAGRAM 2: (Option). 5 picks for 3 and rolls to the basket. 3 can shoot off the pick, pass to 5 on the roll or skip pass to 1 for a corner jumper.

—*Allen Carden, Northwest Whitfield High School, Tunnell Hill, Ga.*

PLAYS FOR GUARDS

GUARD SCISSORS ACTION

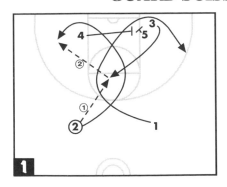

3 breaks to the free-throw line for the pass from 2. The guards (1 and 2) cross out in front and under the basket and come off low post screens from 5 and 4, respectively. 3 can go one-on-one or pass to either side and screen away. The ball side post (4) posts up, then screens for 5.

—*Marty Gillespie,*
Bradley University,
Peoria, Ill.

MOTION CLEAR OUT FOR QUICK GUARD

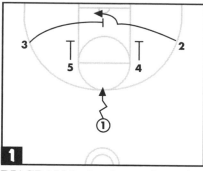

DIAGRAM 1: 2 swings underneath off 3's screen. 5 and 4 screen down.

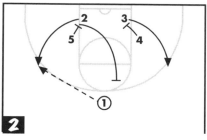

DIAGRAM 2: 1 enters to 2. 5 comes high for the fake back pick on 1 clearing the wing for 2 to operate one-on-one.

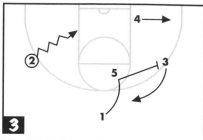

DIAGRAM 3: 4 flares to the short corner. 1 cuts at 5 and screens away on 3.

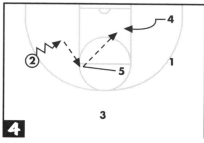

DIAGRAM 4: 4 is ready to board or take a drop off pass on 2's drive. If 2 is jammed or 5's man stays under in help position, 5 breaks to the ball and looks inside to 4.

—Don King, Washington High School, Cedar Rapids, Iowa

INSIDE GUARD SERIES

This inside guard series is a solid man-to-man offense that creates opportunities for all players. This can be used as a continuity offense or a quick hitter, depending on your situation.

DIAGRAM 1: 1 passes to 2. 5 sets a high post screen. 1 uses the screen to look for a return pass for a layup or to post up. 3 rotates to the top for the reversal. 4 drops into the lane and returns to the block.

DIAGRAM 2: If 1 does not receive the pass, 2 reverses the ball to 3. 5 down

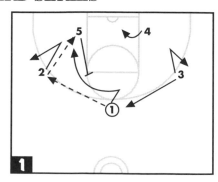

screens for 4, pinning 4's defender.

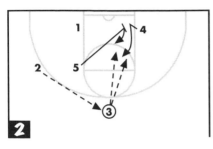

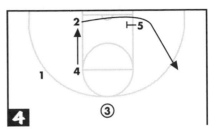

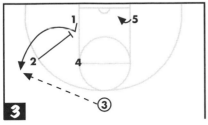

DIAGRAM 3: If 3 does not pass to 4 or 5, 2 screens for 1. 1 pops out to the three-point line for a jump shot or a post up possibility for 2.

DIAGRAM 4: The reset process has 2 move off 5's back screen to the weak side wing. 4 slides from the high post to the low post. 5, 3 and 1 stay at their positions.

—Scott Allen, Kendall High School, Kendall, N.Y.

JUMP SHOT FOR YOUR POINT MAN

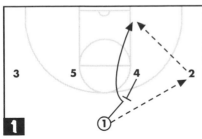

DIAGRAM 1: From the 1-4 offensive set, 1 passes to 2 and runs a vertical cut off 4.

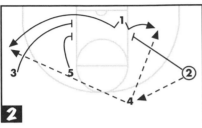

DIAGRAM 2: 2 hits 1 for a layup. If 1 is not open, 4 steps out after screening and 2 passes to 4. On the pass, 3 and 5 set a double screen for 1 and 2 sets a screen for 1 as well. 1 has the option to go either way for the pass from 4 and the jumper.

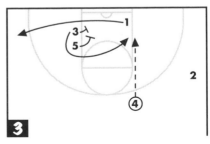

DIAGRAM 3: A great option for this play is to have 2 stay wide after passing to 4. 1 goes off the double screen by 3 and 5, then 3 curls off 5. 4 looks for 3 for a layup. This option is effective against a team that switches on the double screen. You can run it once or twice a game after establishing 1's jump shot.

—Drew Catlett,
Hampden-Sydney College,
Hampden-Sydney, Va.

SET PLAY FOR BEST SHOOTER OR DRIVER

This is a great play to provide your best shooter with a good look at a 10-foot jumper or your best driver with a clear out.

The play is called "Box" and followed by "One" or "Two," depending on which option you want to use.

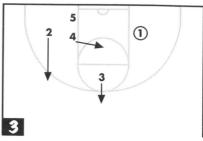

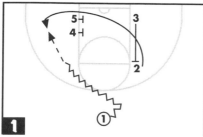

DIAGRAM 1: In the initial set, 5 and 4 set a shoulder-to-shoulder screen on the left low post block, 3 sets up on the right low box and 2 sets up at the right elbow. 1 starts the play at the top of the key and takes a few dribbles to the right before spin-dribbling back to the left. 3 sets a back screen for 2, who makes a direct cut off 3 and around 5 and 4. 1 looks for 2 coming off the double screen.

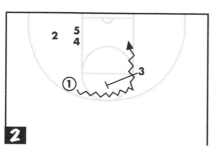

DIAGRAM 2: If 2 is not open, 3 sets a ball screen at the free-throw line for 1. 1 will spin dribble back to the right using the ball screen and drive to the basket.

DIAGRAM 3: As 1 drives to the basket, 3 steps out to act as a safety on defense and 4 steps to the free-throw line to give an option if 1 does not get a shot off. 5 prepares to rebound and 2 steps to the wing.

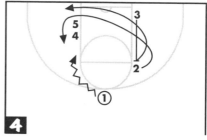

DIAGRAM 4: A second option, called "Box 2," starts with the same initial action. But in this option, 2 continues around and takes a hand off from 1. 3 follows 2 around after setting the back screen.

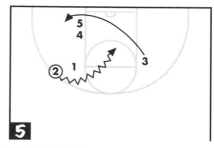

DIAGRAM 5: Now 2 has a clear out after receiving the handoff from 1.

—Larry Trickey,
North Pemiscot High School,
Wardell, Mo.

MOTION PLAY FOR POST PLAYERS

This set play has been very successful for us in getting the ball into our post players.

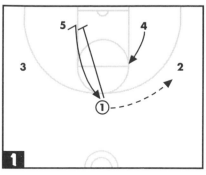

DIAGRAM 1: 1 passes to 2 and screens the opposite post 5. 4 steps up to the elbow.

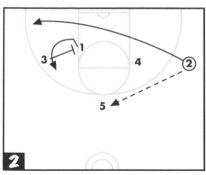

DIAGRAM 2: 2 passes to 5 and clears to the opposite corner. 3 screens down for 1.

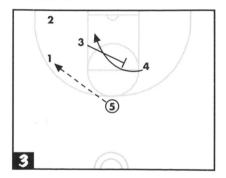

DIAGRAM 3: As 5 swings the ball to 1, 3 sets a diagonal screen for 4.

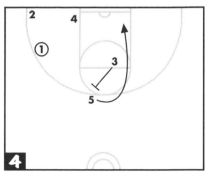

DIAGRAM 4: As 4 clears the screen, 3 will back screen for 5 for a possible lob pass.

DIAGRAM 5: 3 steps out after screening for a possible three-point shot if their defender hedged. On catch by 3, 5 will cross screen for 4 and seal.

—Mitch Mitchell,
Copiah Academy,
Gallman, Miss.

MULTIPLE-OPTION ENTRY PLAY FOR HIGH/LOW MOTION

This play is designed as a specialty play you can use after a free throw attempt, timeout or other stoppage of play. The best feature of this play is that every player on the floor could have a shot attempt.

This play is especially effective if you have a point guard with excellent shooting ability.

The first two options are designed to free the point guard for a good shot attempt, possibly a three-point look.

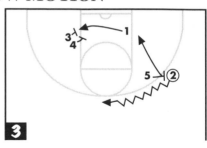

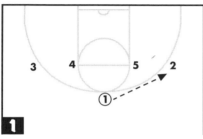

DIAGRAM 1: To initiate the offense, begin in a 1-4 look with 1 passing to a wing (2 or 3).

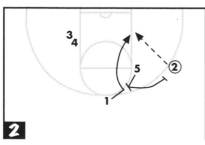

DIAGRAM 2: 1 will cut off a back screen by 5 and look for a post-up pass from 2.

DIAGRAM 3: If the post-up is not there, 2 runs a pick-and-roll with 5. 2 will take the ball to the basket or look for 5, who makes a roll toward the basket.

DIAGRAM 4: 1 holds for a one-count on the block, then cuts off a staggered pick by 4 and 3. 1 must read

their defender and either make a curl cut to the basket or a straight cut to the wing. 1 will receive the pass from 2.

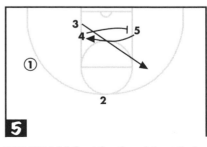

DIAGRAM 5: After 3 and 4 set their picks, 3 fills the spot vacated by 2 and 4 sets a post-post pick for 5 who has rolled to the basket.

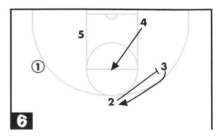

DIAGRAM 6: After 4 sets the pick for 5, 4 rolls to the high post. 2 down screens for 3.
DIAGRAM 7: 2 then pops out at the wing. You are now in a high/low motion game formation in which 4 could receive the pass from 1 and look to 5, who seals. If any of these options are unavailable, simply run your motion set for the remainder of the shot clock.

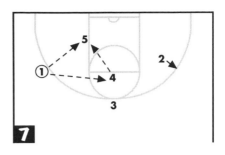

—Jack Mehn, Rainier High School, Rainier, Wash.

MAN OFFENSE TO CREATE MISMATCH

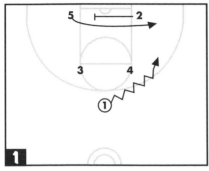

DIAGRAM 1: 1 dribbles to a position opposite 5. 2 screens across, hoping for a switch by the defenders. 1 looks to 5 on the box for a possible post-up scoring opportunity.

DIAGRAM 3: If 2 doesn't have the outside shot, then your team is in a highly valuable screen down, screen across situation.

—Greg Goodwin,
Absegami High School,
Absecon, N.J.

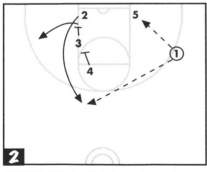

DIAGRAM 2: If 5 doesn't get the ball, 3 and 4 set staggered screens for 2, who comes to the top of the key looking for a jumper or drive.

HIGH/LOW	LOB TO THE BASKET

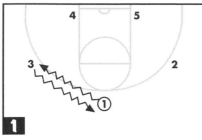

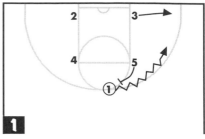

DIAGRAM 1: 1 dribbles toward 3 for a handoff. 3 then dribbles to the top of the key.

DIAGRAM 1: 5 steps out and sets a ball screen for 1 who dribbles to the wing. 3 flashes to the corner.

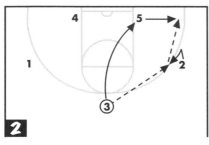

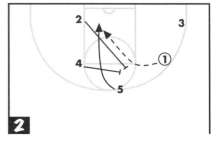

DIAGRAM 2: 3 passes to 2 while 5 pops out to the corner. 2 passes to 5 and 3 replaces 5 in the low post.

DIAGRAM 2: 2 and 4 set a double screen for 5, who breaks to the basket for the lob.

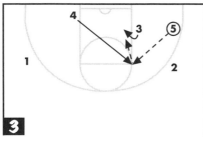

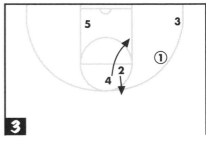

DIAGRAM 3: 4 flashes to the elbow and receives a pass from 5. 4 immediately looks for 3 sealing off the defender.

DIAGRAM 3: If the lob is not there, 2 steps out and 4 flashes to the low post.

—Bill Agronin,
Niagara University,
Niagara University, N.Y.

—Ron Bradley,
Beaver Creek High School,
West Jefferson, N.C.

SET PLAY FOR A MISMATCH

This is a play that incorporates spacing and the opportunity for a mismatch situation needed to give the offense a momentary quick-hitting advantage.

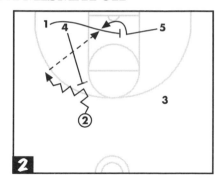

DIAGRAM 1: In 3-out 2-low alignment, both post players (4 and 5) are wide of the lane for spacing and isolation purposes. 1 passes to 2 and cuts to the ball side corner.
DIAGRAM 2: 4 comes up to set a screen on the ball. As 2 dribbles off the screen, 1 cuts across the lane to screen for 5. 2 passes to 5 for a layup.
DIAGRAM 3: If the post up is not there, 4 screens for 1 for a jump shot. 3 spots up on the weak side for a possible skip pass from 2.

—Tom Reiter, Washington & Jefferson College, Washington, Pa.

JUMPER & INSIDE LOOK VS. MAN-TO-MAN

2 is your best jump shooter, 3 your best post-up player. 1 dribbles to the wing. When 1 gets to the wing, 2 screens across for 3, who is 1's first option. As the block-to-block screen occurs, 4 and 5 set a double screen for 2. The play is extremely successful and has worked at all levels (high school, college, pros).

—Barry Parkhill,
William & Mary, Williamsburg, Va.

ALLEY-OOP PLAY

This is a play that requires good timing and a good lob pass.

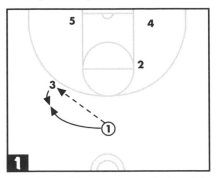

DIAGRAM 1: 1 passes to 3, then follows the pass and gets the ball back from 3.

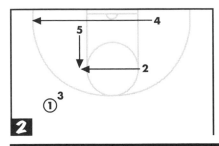

DIAGRAM 2: 2 and 5 come to the ball side elbow and set a double screen for 3. 4 goes to the ball side corner and calls for the ball.

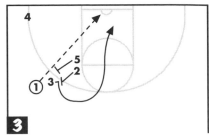

DIAGRAM 3: 3 rubs their defender off the double screen and goes to the basket. 1 lobs a pass toward the basket for a dunk or easy layup. This play works for us when we face a team that likes to overplay and deny the ball in the passing lanes.

—Brad Ballou,
Blue Hill High School,
Blue Hill, Neb.

HIGH POST PLAY

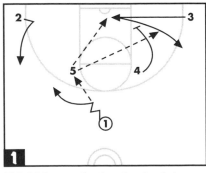

This high post play is quite simple but very difficult to defend. 1 brings the ball downcourt and bounce-passes to the high post man (5), hitting them on their outside hand. 5 pivots on the inside foot to face the basket. 3 walks their defender into the lane and straddles the lane while 4 turns outside and head hunts 3's defender. Meanwhile, 1 and 2 do a loose split off the high post to keep their defenders out of the lane. 3 reads the defense and either steps to the basket for the short jumper or pops out to the wing off the down pick. When 3 gets the ball at the wing, they can usually take one or two quick dribbles and get off a great shot or feed the post player on the block.

—Bill Morse,
Fort Hays State University,
Hays, Kan.

INSIDE/OUTSIDE SCORING PLAY

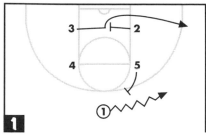

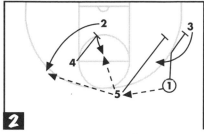

DIAGRAM 1: 2 (your best outside threat) screens for 3 (decoy) as 1 dribbles off 5's ball screen.

DIAGRAM 2: 1 quickly reverses the ball to 5, while 4 (your best inside threat) screens down for 2. After passing, 1 and 5 set a staggered screen for

3. This action is a very effective two-player isolation play for 2 and 4.

—Will Rey,
Loyola University,
Chicago, Ill.

RANDOM PLAYS

SEAHAWK VS. MAN-TO-MAN

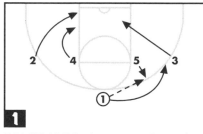

DIAGRAM 1: 1 passes to 5 stepping out. 2 and 4 move down to set a stagger screen for 3 cutting around to the weak side. 1 follows the pass for a fake handoff.

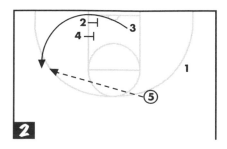

DIAGRAM 2: 3 comes around the double screen and receives a pass from 5.

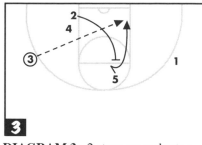

DIAGRAM 3: 2 steps up and sets a back screen for 5. 3 throws a lob pass to 5.

—Lason Perkins,
Cary High School,
Cary, N.C.

GEORGETOWN

Run this play to get a quick two points off a back screen, or get the same player a three-point shot off of the screen for the screener action.

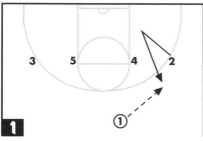

DIAGRAM 1: Start in a 1-4 set with the two post players at the elbows of the foul line. 1 passes to 2 after 2 executes a V-cut.

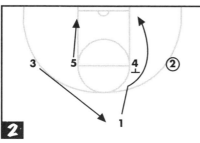

DIAGRAM 2: 4 sets a back screen for 1. 5 cuts to the opposite block and 3 cuts to the top of the key.

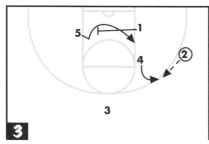

DIAGRAM 3: If 1 does not receive the ball off the back screen, 1 then sets a pick for 5. 4 pops out to the ball to receive the pass from 2.
DIAGRAM 4: As soon as 1 sets the

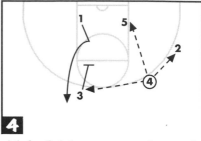

pick for 5, 1 then cuts up to the top of the key off the screen from 3. 4 can pass to 5, 1 or back to 2.

—Jimmy Brown,
Georgia Southern,
Statesboro, Ga.

STAGGERED STACKS POP-UP

This play has several options. 1 dribbles down and passes to 2, who pops to the middle. 2 can now pass to: 1 on an alley-oop cut off 5; 5 on a duck-in after a back screen for 1; or 3 coming off a screen by 4.

—Murray Arnold,
Western Kentucky University,
Bowling Green, Ky.

SPREAD

"SIDE TWO" OR "SIDE THREE"

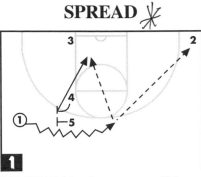

DIAGRAM 1: 1 penetrates off the double screen looking for 4 rolling to the basket or 2 if their defender comes to help on penetration.

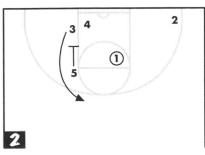

DIAGRAM 2: 3 uses a screen from 5 to spot up for a three-point shot behind 1's penetration.

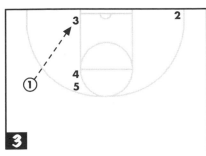

DIAGRAM 3: You can also use the spread formation to isolate 3 in the post.

—Nevin Gleddie,
University College of the Cariboo,
Kamloops, B.C., Canada

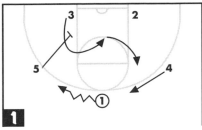

DIAGRAM 1: 3 curls off 5's screen into the lane and out. 4 moves toward 1 as 1 dribbles to the left.

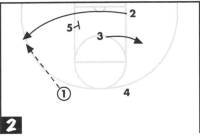

DIAGRAM 2: 2 comes off 5's screen and looks for the shot in the corner or a pass to 5 in the post.

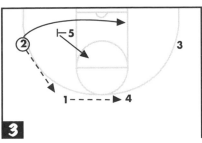

DIAGRAM 3: The offense resets as 2 passes back to 1, who passes to 4 at the top. The same inside and outside passing options are available as in the previous option. 5's cut back into position resets baseline continuity.

—Fran Fraschilla,
St. John's University,
Jamaica, N.Y.

3-2 OFFENSE THAT GIVES OPPONENTS FITS

Numerous articles have been written on continuity offenses and their ability to give opponents fits. As a coach for many years, I am a believer in implementing a continuity offense and its sets.

DIAGRAM 1: 1 passes to 3 off the V-cut. 2 back screens for 5, who looks to face out.

your team can score quickly or run the shot clock down and get a good look at the basket with the ball in the hands of the player you want to run the offense.

—Bill Horn,
Arkport Central High School,
Arkport, N.Y.

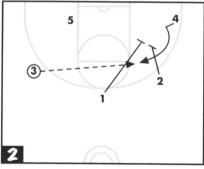

DIAGRAM 2: 3 holds the ball while 1 and 2 set staggered screens for 4 coming to the elbow. 3 passes to 4.
DIAGRAM 3: 4 passes to 1, who has popped out to the wing. 2 sets a back screen for 3, then sets a screen for 5 before popping out to the perimeter. Now you are back in the beginning set.

The continuity offense can be structured or be as loose as you want to make it. Each and every offense has its strengths and weaknesses. You will find that by implementing this offense,

TWIST PLAY

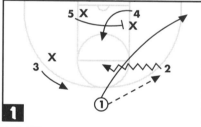

DIAGRAM 1: 1 passes to 2 and cuts to the ball side corner. 2 drives ball to the middle of the free-throw line while 3 spots up for a three-point shot. 4 posts-up for a two-second count, then turns baseline and button hooks back to receive the ball. 5 picks their defender on flash across the lane and back picks 4's defender at the same time. 2 hits 4 for a layup. If 3's defender drops to help, 3 is open for the three-point attempt.

—Marc Comstock,
Emporia State University,
Emporia, Kan.

CARDINAL

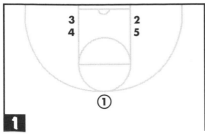

DIAGRAM 1: Players start off in a double stack with post players on the block.

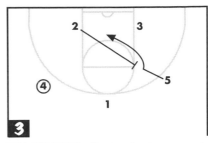

DIAGRAM 3: 2 sets a back screen at the elbow. 5 goes off the back screen and posts-up.

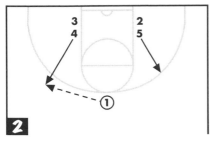

DIAGRAM 2: 4 and 5 pop out to the free-throw line extended. 1 passes to 4 or 5. This shows 4 receiving the pass.

DIAGRAM 4: 1 and 2 set a staggered screen for 3, who looks for the three-point shot.

—Mike Feagans, West Lafayette High School, West Lafayette, Ind.

15 PLAY WITH THREE OPTIONS

5 sets a ball screen for 1, then rolls to the basket. 3 breaks off a double screen by 4 and 2. After screening, 4 flashes to the ball and 2 flashes to the corner.

OPTION 1: 1 shoots off 5's screen.

OPTION 2: 3 has a great shot coming off the double screen.

OPTION 3: 4 takes the shot after flashing to the middle. The play is called "15" because 5 picks for 1.

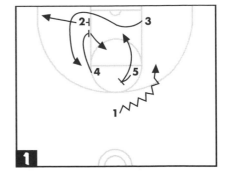

—Van Chancellor, University of Mississippi, Oxford, Miss.

CAROLINA VS. MAN

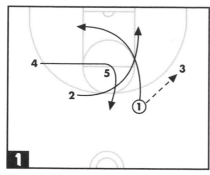

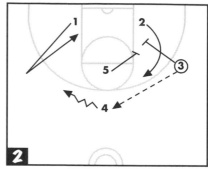

DIAGRAM 1: From a 2-3 set, 1 hits 3 on the wing and makes a cut to the basket. When the pass is made, 2 cuts behind 1 to the ball side post position as 4 cuts into the lane and out to the top of 5's position.

DIAGRAM 2: 3 reverses the ball to 4 and sets a down screen for 2. With the ball in 4's hands, 1 pops out and cuts back door. 5 sets a second screen for 2 cutting to the top. 4 can hit either 1 on the back door cut or 2 popping out.

—Lason Perkins, Cary High School, Cary, N.C.

OPEN VS. MAN-TO-MAN

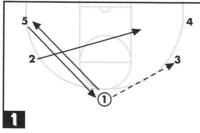

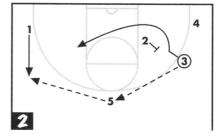

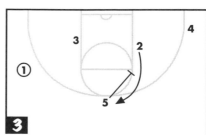

DIAGRAM 1: 1 passes to 3 on the wing then cuts to the opposite corner. 2 cuts to the mid-post area as 5 cuts to the top to fill the vacant spot.

DIAGRAM 2: 3 reverses to 5, who passes to 1. After the pass, 3 runs their defender off 2's screen and continues to the basket.

DIAGRAM 3: After passing to 1, 5 screens 2's defender as 2 pops to the top of the key. 1 looks to pass to 3 on the post up or 2 for the jump shot.

—Lason Perkins, Cary High School, Cary, N.C.

TRIANGLE OFFENSE COMPLEMENT

This play complements the triangle offense and is used in a traditional alignment for modern play. Its strengths include the ability to finish with a top of the key three-point shot. It also establishes an inside game to balance the offensive attack.

The play's keys are hard cuts and correct passing decisions.

screen for 1 and 2. 5 passes to 2 (or 1).

DIAGRAM 4: 3 sets a diagonal screen for 4. 5 sets a down screen for 3. 4 posts at ball side block.

—Craig Jonas,
Coach's Edge,
Lawrence, Kan.

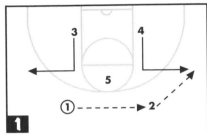

DIAGRAM 1: 4 and 3 L-cut up and out as 1 swings the ball to 2. 2 enters to 4. Entering to 3 is another possibility. Spacing is important.

SCREEN THE SCREENER

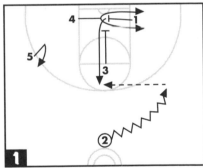

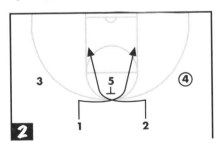

DIAGRAM 2: Passer cuts first. Be aware of the skip-pass possibilities.

2 dribbles the ball toward the side of 1. 1 sets a screen across the lane for 4 simultaneously as 3 comes down the lane to set a screen for 1. Timing is very important. If properly executed, 1 should get a jump shot between the top of the circle and the free-throw line. 5 occupies their defender. 4 can be open if the defense falls asleep.

—Don Sicko,
University of Detroit,
Detroit, Mich.

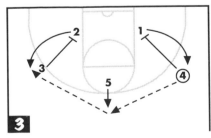

DIAGRAM 3: 4 passes to 5. 4 and 3

WAKE FOREST VS. MAN-TO-MAN

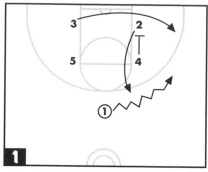

DIAGRAM 1: 1 dribbles to the right. 3 cuts across the lane to the corner as 4 screens for 2.

DIAGRAM 2: 1 passes to 2. 2 dribbles over as 5 moves down the lane and posts up for a shot.

—Lason Perkins, Cary High School, Cary, N.C.

"GEORGETOWN" PLAY FOR A CORNER JUMPER

This play, which we call "Georgetown," is designed for a hot or good corner jump-shooter. This play can be run to either side.

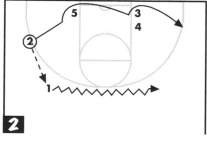

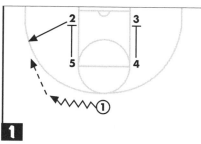

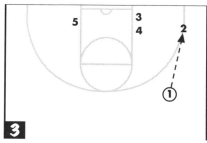

DIAGRAM 1: 1 calls the name of the player who'll get the shot (2 in this case) and dribbles to that side. 2 comes off the down screen by 5 to receive the pass from 1. 4 down screens for 3 at the same time.

DIAGRAM 2: 2 catches the pass and faces the basket before passing back to 1. 2 then cuts off a pick set by 5 and a double pick by 3 and 4 and goes to the right corner. 1 reverses dribble and goes right.

DIAGRAM 3: 1 looks off before passing to 2 for the corner jumper.

—Pete Lasavage,
Akiba Hebrew Academy,
Merion Station, Pa.

HEAD TAP

This box set can be run as a sideline play from out-of-bounds. The play's strengths include its quick hitting ability and secondary three-point opportunity. The keys to its success are timing and solid screening.

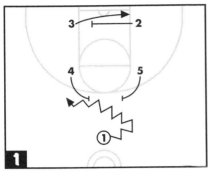

DIAGRAM 1: 1 can go either way (preferably opposite best shooter). 2 screens across for 3. 5 or 4 are available for ball screens.

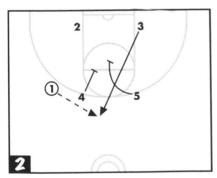

DIAGRAM 2: 5 and 4 stagger their screens for 3. (3 should read the defense, they can curl around the screens as well.) 2 posts up.

DIAGRAM 3: 5 V-cuts out, then back to ball screen for 3; screen and roll. 4 and 1 set true double screen for 2.

DIAGRAM 4: 3 and 5 have screen and roll or two-player game. Mini top of key skip pass can be made from 3 to 2. 4 is open inside after 1 sprints out high.

—Craig Jonas,
Coach's Edge,
Andover, Kan.

LOOKOUT

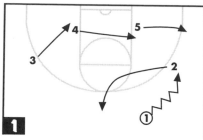

DIAGRAM 1: 1 dribbles to wing, 2 loops and 5 pops out to the wing. 4 cuts to the ball side low post and 3 moves to the weak side low post.

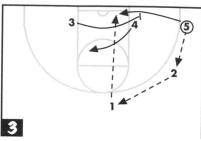

DIAGRAM 3: 5 passes to 2 and 2 passes to 1. 4 flashes to the dotted line, 3 screens opposite and 5 cuts back door for a possible pass and dunk.

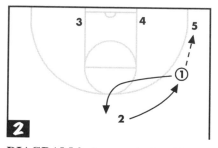

DIAGRAM 2: 1 passes to 5 and loops out. 2 replaces 1.

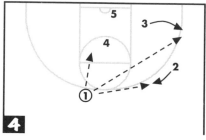

DIAGRAM 4: 1 can also pass to 4 flashing to the middle, or to 2 or 3 for the three-point shot.

—Bob Rhodin, Fletcher High School, Neptune Beach, Fla.

A PLAY TO SAVE THE DAY!

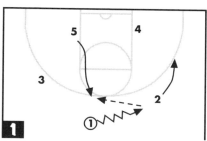

DIAGRAM 1: 1 dribbles over and passes to 5, who pops out. 3 should be your best outside shooter.
DIAGRAM 2: 2 scoops off 4's pick and goes to the basket for the pass from 5.

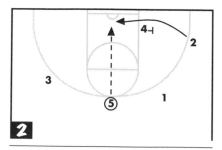

—Dean Hollingsworth, Rockdale High School, Rockdale, Texas

SPECIAL PLAY CALL VS. MAN DEFENSE

This is a special play call we have been using for several years and many area coaches are now running the play themselves. At least one of the options is always open at some time during the play.

DIAGRAM 2: 4's defender will have a tendency to help on 2, so 4 comes off the double-staggered screen for a three-pointer at the top of the key.

DIAGRAM 3: If 4 does not have a shot, 4 reverses the ball to 1.

DIAGRAM 1: In this set, 2 would be your best scorer and 4 would be your best shooting big player. 1 enters the ball into 3. 5 screens away for 2.

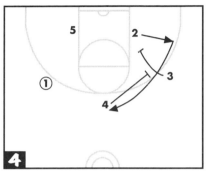

DIAGRAM 4: Now 1 and 5 have a two-player game. Meanwhile, 2 comes off a double staggered pick set by 4 and 3.

—Mark Graupe,
Central Middle School,
Devils Lake, N.D.

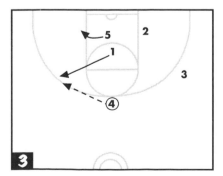

"POWER" VS. MAN-TO-MAN

DIAGRAM 1: 1 dribbles to the wing. 2 sets a diagonal screen for 4, then continues up the lane for ball reversal. 1 looks for 4, who posts up hard. If 5's defender helps out on 4, then 1 can go to 5 for high-low action or 3 on the duck in.

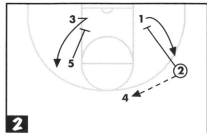

DIAGRAM 2: If 4 is guarded, 1 reverses the ball to 2, who dribbles to the opposite wing. As this occurs, 3 sets a diagonal screen for 5 and continues up the lane for floor balance.

DIAGRAM 3: If 5 is guarded, 2 reverses the ball to 3. You're now in a 1-2-2 set and can begin most man-to-man offenses.

—Kyle Haney, Holmes High School, Covington, Ky.

SET PLAY (MIAMI)

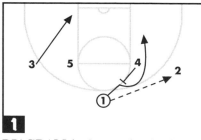

DIAGRAM 1: 1 starts the play by passing to 2, then makes a high post cut off a screen from 4. At the same time, 3 takes their defender to the baseline.

DIAGRAM 2: If 1 is not open, 2 passes to 4 and screens for 1 as 5

screens for 3. 4 has the option to pass to either 1 or 3.

—Joe Pitt, Union High School, Union, S.C.

PACER VS. MAN-TO-MAN

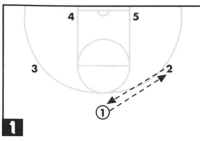

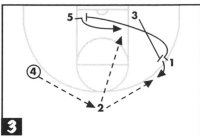

DIAGRAM 1: 1 passes to 2, who looks for 5 in the post. If 5 isn't open, 2 passes back to 1.

DIAGRAM 2: On the pass from 2 to 1, 4 steps out and back picks 3. 1 passes to 4, who looks for 5 coming across the lane off a screen by 3. 1 and 2 can either exchange or screen for each other.
DIAGRAM 3: If 4 has no pass to 5, 4 passes to 2. 3 then back picks 1. 2 passes to 3 or 5 coming off a screen in the lane set by 1.

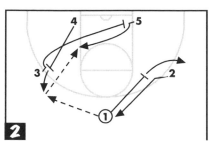

*—Lason Perkins,
Cary High School, Cary, N.C.*

A SPECIAL PLAY TO SCORE

DIAGRAM 1: 1 dribbles to either wing area (right side shown), clearing out that player. At the same time, 5 goes across the lane to set a screen for 4. 3 and 2 then set a double screen for 4, who comes off the screens until open for a jump shot. 4 also can go all the way out to the three-point area for the shot.

DIAGRAM 2: If there's no shot, 4 looks for 2 sealing off their defender in the lane or for 3 drifting out to the three-point area for a shot.

*—Bill Agronin,
Niagara University,
Niagara University, N.Y.*

"CAROLINA PLAY"

This play offers numerous options, and as your players become more comfortable with it, they may find some of their own.

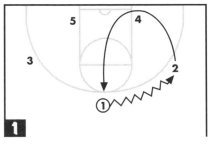

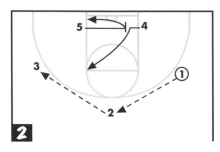

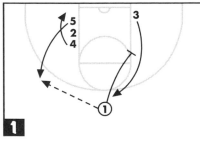

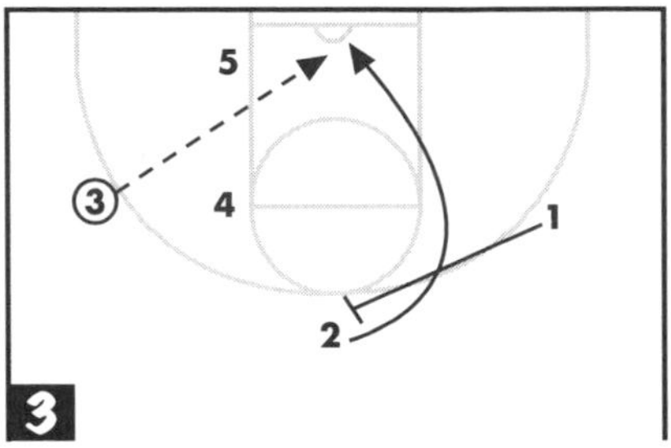

DIAGRAM 1: From the basic set, 1 dribble enters to the right wing. 2 comes around 4 and replaces 1 at the point.

DIAGRAM 2: The ball is reversed from 1 to 2 to 3. When the ball reaches 3, 5 screens across for 4, who comes to the high post. After setting the screen, 5 comes back hard to the low post.

DIAGRAM 3: After 4 and 5 overload the ball side of the floor, 1 sets a back screen for 2, who breaks to the basket for the back door pass from 3.

—Rick Berger,
Westfield State College,
Westfield, Mass.

POP AND SHUFFLE

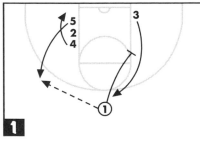

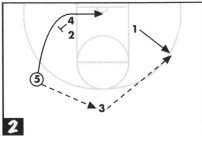

DIAGRAM 1: 5 pops out and receives the pass from 1. 2 back picks for 4, who cuts down the lane. 1 screens away for 3, who goes to the top.

DIAGRAM 2: 3 receives the pass from 5. If they choose to reverse the ball, then 5 shuffle cuts off a screen by 4. If they choose not to reverse, then 4 or 2 are the logical receivers.

—Sonny Smith, Auburn University, Auburn, Ala.

1-2-2 CONTINUITY PLAY

This 1-2-2 continuity play can give you some great shot options.

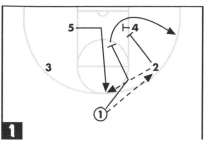

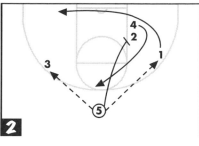

DIAGRAM 1: 1 hits 2 with a pass, then cuts toward the elbow and screens diagonally for 5 coming to the top. 2 passes to 5 and screens down for 1, who then comes off the double screen set by 2 and 4.

DIAGRAM 2: 5 has the ball on top. 5 can pass to 1 or 3. If passed to 3, then 1 cuts off the double screen set by 2 and 4 to the strong side block. 5 then screens down for 4 coming to the top, cutting off the double screen set by 5 and 2.

DIAGRAM 3: Now you're back in the continuity again. This play is a good combination of diagonal screens and wheel action.

—Sonny Smith,
Auburn University,
Auburn, Ala.

SCREEN-THE-SCREENER: VARIATION

This is a wrinkle off the screen-the-screener play. 2 dribbles to the wing. 1 screens for 4. 3 fakes the screen down for 1 and returns. 1 continues out of the lane opposite the ball. 2 reverses the ball to 3. 5 down screens for 1. 3 hits 1 for a jumper.

—Don Sicko,
University of Detroit,
Detroit, Mich.

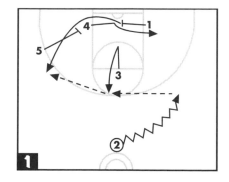

SECONDARY OPTIONS OFF FAST BREAK

There are two basic components to the fast break: primary and secondary. The primary break is looking for the layup or high-percentage shot before the defense can get set. Both the primary and secondary fast break objectives are to achieve a numerical advantage.

Here are two ways to run the secondary break. Both result in good shots and potential mismatches that put an enormous strain on the defense.

DIAGRAM 1: 1 is the primary ball handler. 2 is the second guard and best shooter. 1's responsibility is to get the ball to 2 for the quick shot. If 2 isn't available, the secondary phase is entered as 2 passes back to 1. 2 and 3 flatten out along the baseline.

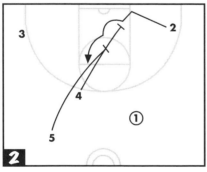

DIAGRAM 2: 4 is the trailer in the play (4 and 5 are interchangeable.) 4 and 5 set staggered screens for 2. 5 should take a position approximately 8

to 10 feet behind 4. 4 and 5 should flash to the ball after setting the staggered screen and try to force a defensive switch.

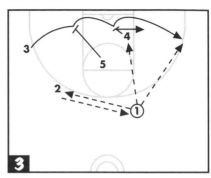

DIAGRAM 3: 4 and 5 move to opposite blocks after setting the screen for 2. 3 moves to the mid-post extended. 1 passes to 2, who reverses the ball back to 1. During the reversal, 3 comes off the baseline screens of 4 and 5. 1 passes to 4 at the ball side block or to 3 off the cut.

DIAGRAM 4: The second option starts basically the same way. 1 tries to push the ball to 2. The difference here is that 3's primary concern is to get to the ball side block and look for a post up off either the 1 to 3 or 2 to 3 pass. If 3 sprints the floor, easy baskets could result. 4 and 5 are the trailers.

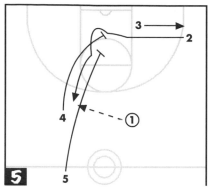

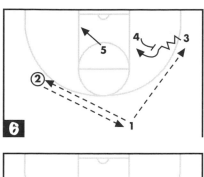

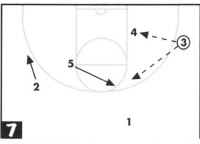

DIAGRAM 5: 4, the first trailer, comes into the lane with 5 trailing by 10 to 12 feet. 2 comes off the staggered screen by 4 and 5. 3 moves out to the corner.

DIAGRAM 6: If the shot by 2 is not open, the passes go from 2 to 1 to 3 in the corner. 4, in this case, sees 3 does not have a shot and moves out to engage a pick and roll play.

DIAGRAM 7: 4 can post up low with 5 moving over to receive the pass to initiate the high-low action.

—Rick Walrond, Bethune-Cookman College, Daytona Beach, Fla.

THREE OPTIONS OFF THE FAST BREAK

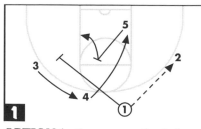

OPTION 1: 5 up screens for 4, then releases to the weak side block. 1 hits 2 on the strong side wing. 1 screens away to 3 on the weak side wing.

OPTION 2: 5 screens for 3, who can go high or low, depending on how they're being defended. 2 picks for 1. 1 hits the trailer 4.

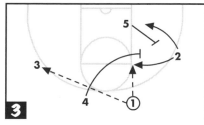

OPTION 3: 4 and 5 screen for 2, who cuts high or low, depending on their defender. If 2's not open, 1 hits 3 on the weak side wing.

—John Gibson, University of Tennessee-Chattanooga, Chattanooga, Tenn.

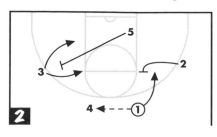

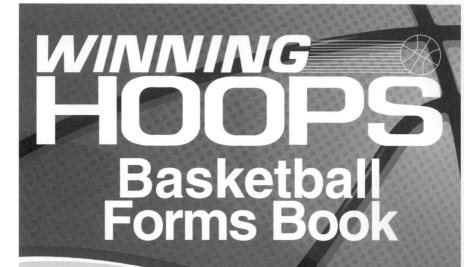

WINNING HOOPS
Basketball Forms Book

Foreword written by Shaka Smart! Organize. Save time. Improve record keeping. Train assistants. Make decisions. Win more games.

PLUS each book includes a forms CD — ABSOLUTELY FREE — with all 93 forms and templates to print whenever you need them.

Price includes CD.
Only $34.95.

Call 616-887-9008, ext. 115, to order.
Visit www.winninghoops.com.

Chapter 6

PLAYS TO START SPECIFIC OFFENSES

BOX SETS

BOX SET PLAYS

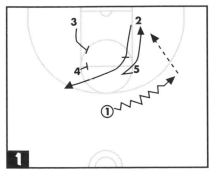

DIAGRAM 1: As 1 dribbles over to 5's side, 2 back screens for 5 and 1 looks for the bounce pass to 5. Meanwhile, 3 and 4 are setting up for a double-flair screen.

DIAGRAM 2: If 1 sees 2's defender helping on the back screen for 5, 1 reverses the dribble, looks at the basket to freeze the defense and finds 2 coming off the flare screen.

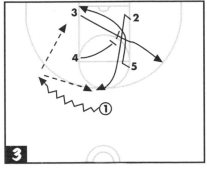

DIAGRAM 3: As 1 dribbles to the left side, 3 sets a screen for 5 to get open in the post. Simultaneously, 4 is setting a screen for 2 to set up an open jumper at the top of the key.

The confusion of the screens being set at the same time makes this play hard to defend. If 2 is unable to get a shot off and 5 isn't open, look to reverse the ball to 3 for penetration, a shot or a pass into 4 who sealed their defender. If you still don't have anything, you are left in a three-out, two-in formation.

—Brent Lemond,
Vanguard High School,
Ocala, Fla.

BOX SET PLAYS

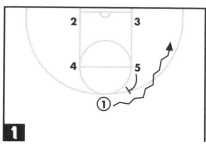

DIAGRAM 1: 1 dribbles to either side to begin motion. 5 steps out to screen for 1.

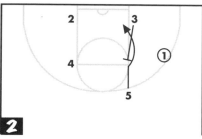

DIAGRAM 2: After 1 moves to the wing, 3 steps out to screen for 5. 5 cuts to the basket.

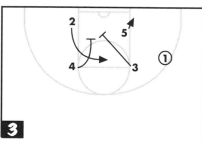

DIAGRAM 3: If a pass to 5 is not open, 4 and 3 double screen for 2, who flashes into the lane. 5 keeps position in low block. 1 can feed 2 off the cut or try and find 5 cutting away from the basket.

—*Ron Bradley,
Beaver Creek High School,
West Jefferson, N.C.*

FLEX BOX VS. MAN-TO-MAN

DIAGRAM 1: 1 dribbles to the side as 3 steps up and picks for 5.

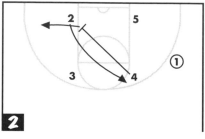

DIAGRAM 2: As 5 is posting, 4 screens for 2.

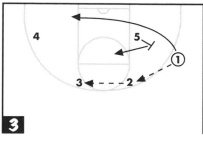

DIAGRAM 3: 1 can make a pass to 5 or reverse the ball to 2. On the reversal, 1 makes a flex cut off 5.

—*Lason Perkins,
Cary High School,
Cary, N.C.*

MAN-TO-MAN BOX SET PLAY

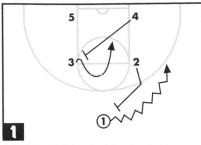

DIAGRAM 2: If 3 doesn't get the pass, 3 screens for 5, who comes off the screen looking for a pass from 1.

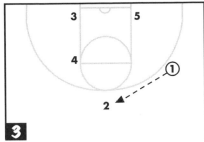

DIAGRAM 1: 2 picks for 1, who dribbles to the right wing. At the same time, 4 picks for 3. 3 comes off 4's screen and looks for a pass from 1.

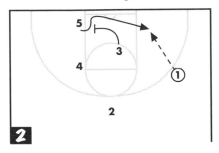

DIAGRAM 3: If 5 doesn't get the ball, 1 passes to 2 at the point. Then you can run the play to the left side.

—David Catanzaro,
West Branch Junior-Senior High School,
Morrisdale, Pa.

BACK DOOR PLAY FROM THE BOX SET

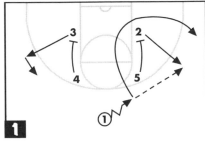

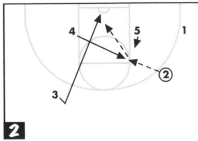

DIAGRAM 1: 4 and 5 screen down to allow 3 and 2 to pop out to the wings. 1 cuts to the strong side corner after passing to 2. 3 begins to set up the defender by starting to the top of the key.

DIAGRAM 2: 2 looks to the corner and 4 flashes to the ball. (If denied, 4 plants and goes back door for the lob). 3 makes a direct cut to the basket as 4 catches the ball. 4 turns to make a bounce pass to 3. If 3 is denied, 4 turns back to feed 5, who has pinned their defender.

—Thom Sigel, Galesburg High School, Galesburg, Ill.

BOX DRIBBLE

This play is designed to isolate the post for a mismatch situation.

RIGHT

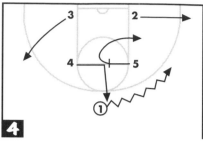

LEFT

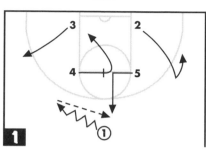

DIAGRAM 1: 1 dribbles to the left to initiate the play. 4 screens across for 5, who pops out to the top of the key. 4 then peels off to the block. 3 comes to the wing, 2 V-cuts to the strong side wing.

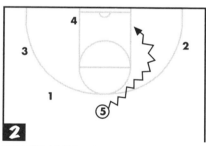

DIAGRAM 2: 5 takes defender to the basket to try and draw a foul and a three-point play.

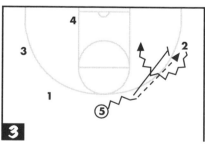

DIAGRAM 3: 5 can kick the ball to 2 and play pick and roll.

DIAGRAM 4: 1 dribbles to the right to initiate the play. 5 screens across for 4, who pops to the top of the key. 5 peels back to the block. 2 fades to the corner and 3 pops out to the wing.

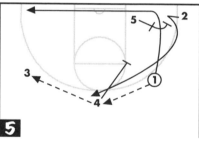

DIAGRAM 5: 1 reverses the ball to 4 who passes to 3. 1 cuts to the far corner off a screen by 5. 5 and 4 then set a staggered double screen for 2 who comes to the top of the key.

DIAGRAM 6: 3 passes the ball to 2 for the jumper to initiate your regular offense.

—Andy Manning,
Jacksonville University, Jacksonville, Fla.

STACK ENTRY TO FLEX

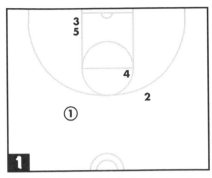

DIAGRAM 1: This is the basic set.

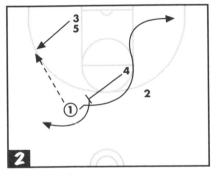

DIAGRAM 2: 3 pops out to the wing to take the entry pass from 1. 5 posts low, 4 back screens for 1, who cuts to the basket and continues to the corner.

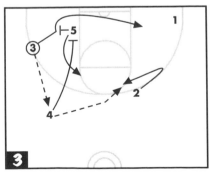

DIAGRAM 3: After screening, 4 steps out to receive the pass from 3. 4 reverses the ball to 2, who cuts back to the ball. 3 runs a baseline flex cut. 4

screens for 5, who comes to the elbow in the basic flex.

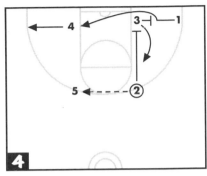

DIAGRAM 4: 1 runs a baseline cut off 3's screen. 2 reverses the ball to 5, then screens for 3. 3 pops up to the elbow. 4 jumps to the corner.

—Rick Berger,
Westfield State, Westfield, Mass.

STRONG SIDE FLEX OPTION

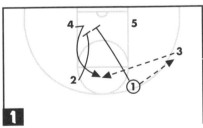

This play is an option off the pass to the strong side in the flex. If 1 passes the ball to 3 (to the strong side), 1 and 2 crack down and set a double screen for 4, who looks for the jumper or dumps down to 5.

—Ron Righter,
University of Southern California,
Los Angeles, Calif.

FLEX IN A 1-4 ALIGNMENT

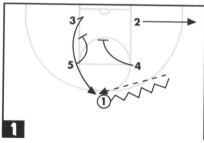

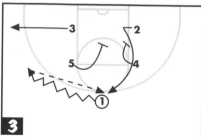

DIAGRAM 1: 1 dribbles right. 2 pops out to the strong side corner. 5 and 4 set a staggered screen for 3. 1 reverses to 3.

DIAGRAM 3: Here is the same play from the opposite direction. 1 dribbles left. 3 pops out to the strong side corner. 4 and 5 set a staggered screen for 2. 1 reverses to 2.

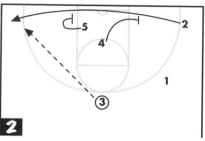

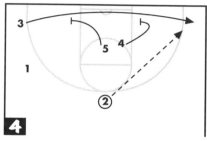

DIAGRAM 2: 2 gets a screen on the strong side block from 4 and on the weak side block from 5. 2 cuts to the opposite corner for the pass and shot.

DIAGRAM 4: 4 and 5 screen on the weak side and strong side blocks, respectively, to set up 3's shot.

—Mack McCarthy, Virginia Commonwealth University, Richmond, Va.

FLEX OFFENSE OPTION

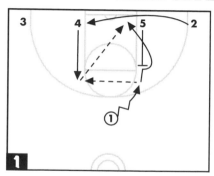

This is an option play that goes well with a flex offense. 1 dribbles to the side, then passes across to 4 coming out. Instead of 1 screening for 5, 5 sets a back screen for 1. 4 throws a lob for 1. This play works best if the point guard (1) is a great leaper.

—Charles Coles,
Central Michigan University,
Mt. Pleasant, Mich.

SET PLAY INTO 1-2-2 MOTION OFFENSE SET

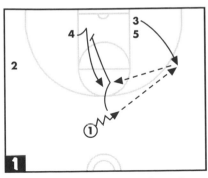

DIAGRAM 1: 1 passes to 3 coming out of the stack. 1 then screens down for 4, who comes to the top to get the pass from 3.

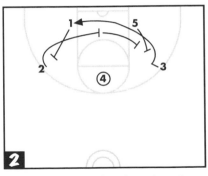

DIAGRAM 2: When 4 receives the pass, 1 back screens for 2 and 5 back screens for 3. If 2 is not open off the initial screen, 2 continues across the lane to screen for 3 and then for 5.

DIAGRAM 3: 5 curls off that screen, creating the 1-2-2 motion offense set.

Coaching point: 2 must be careful not to set a moving screen, and to get out of the lane to avoid a three-second violation. This play will work especially well if 4 is a solid 14- to 17-foot jump shooter.

—Michael McBride,
The Basketball Office,
Clarksville, Ind.

LOBO

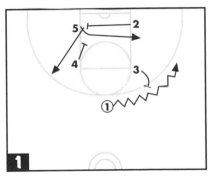

1 dribbles over and receives a ball screen from 3. 2 sets a cross pick for 5 for our first option. 4 sets a down pick for 2 for our second option. If nothing is open, we kick right into our motion offense.

—Joe Pitt,
Union High School,
Union, S.C.

1-3-1 MULTIPURPOSE OFFENSE

This offense can be used against man-to-man, zone or box-and-one defenses. If it is used against a box-and-one defense, 4 must be the player defended man-to-man.

DIAGRAM 1: 1 dribbles in either direction, preferably away from 4. This takes away the entry pass, which can cause some problems.

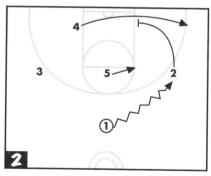

DIAGRAM 2: 2 goes to the low block to screen for 4, who breaks to the corner. 5 goes to the ball side elbow.

DIAGRAM 3: 3 covers weak side rebounding. 1 can pass the ball to 4 for a shot. 5 pops out to the top of the key. 2 sets a screen for 4, then releases to the opposite wing while 3 is setting screens for 2 and 4. 5 rolls to the ball side elbow. 1 covers weak side rebounding.

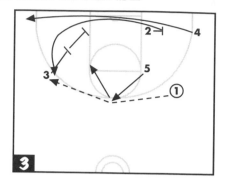

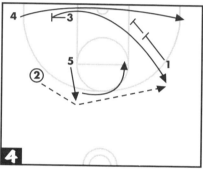

DIAGRAM 4: Ball is reversed to 5, who pops out to receive a pass from 2. 3 screens for 4, then releases to the opposite wing. 1 sets screens for 3 and 4, who continues along the baseline. 2 maintains position for weak side rebounding.

Note: This offense is effective when you don't have a good center, but have a decent shooter with other players who can pass, screen and move.

It is most effective if the center can shoot from 12 to 15 feet and can handle the ball. The benefits of the offense are 1, 2 and 3 are interchangeable (basically running the same pattern) and the entry pass from the point to the wing is eliminated.

—Keith Siefkes,
Beth Eden Baptist School,
Denver, Colo.

"TROUBLE OFFENSE"

This offense is designed to bring continual movement into the offensive attack and present the defense with many obstacles. The offense gives you isolation in the post, creates one-on-one opportunities, sends cutters off double screens and opens players on the weak side.

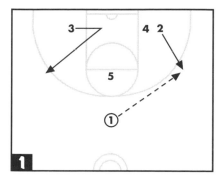

DIAGRAM 1: The ball can be entered from either wing. Shown is an entry from the strong side to 2, who jab steps and breaks from the baseline. 3 does the same at the other wing.

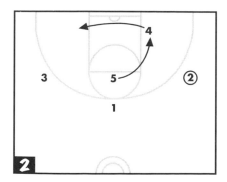

DIAGRAM 2: If 4 does not get position at the low post, 4 should clear with 5 breaking down the lane to make room for a pass and post-up score. 5's defender will be sealed if they aren't in proper position.

DIAGRAM 3: When 5 reaches the low post, 4 cuts back looking for the ball. 5 can use 4 as a screen to get off a shot. 1 sets a down screen for 3 while 4 is cutting back. 3 cuts to the top of the key looking for the reverse from 2.

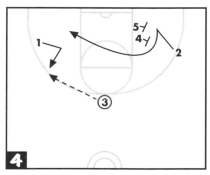

DIAGRAM 4: 3 immediately swings the ball to 1, who looks for a one-on-one or for 2 cutting off the double screen by 5 and 4. 2 stops at the box to post up.

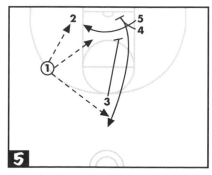

DIAGRAM 5: 5 cuts across the lane

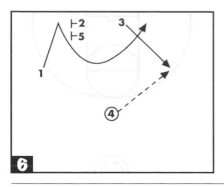

looking for the ball. 3 sets a down screen for 4, who cuts to the point looking for a reverse pass.

DIAGRAM 6: 4 immediately swings the ball to 3. 1 cuts off the double screen by 2 and 5.

Keys to Offense: Constant movement, solid down screens and all players get into the offense and find offensive opportunities.

—*John Pretzer, Edmore High School, Edmore, N.D.*

Chapter 7

LAST SECOND PLAYS

MAN X

PLAYS FOR OPEN SHOTS

LAST SECOND TOURNAMENT SHOT

This play is easy to teach and run. It has five basic options that can turn into many more with different pass combinations. It takes about eight seconds to run if you have to go through all the options.

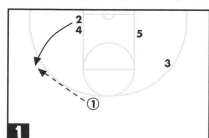

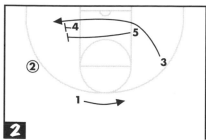

DIAGRAM 1: 2 pops out for a pass from 1 and a possible shot opportunity (option 1).

DIAGRAM 2: 5 cuts across the lane and sets a double screen with 4 for a shot opportunity by 3 (option 2).

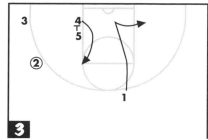

DIAGRAM 3: If 3 doesn't get a pass from 2, 4 pops to the elbow off 5's screen (option 3). 1 cuts to the basket as a rebounder. 2 may also pass down to 5 (option 4).

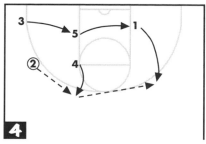

DIAGRAM 4: If none of this is available on this overload, 4 pops out to reverse the ball to 1 for a shot (option 5).

—Ric Franklin,
Victory Christian Academy,
Gastonia, N.C.

LAST SECOND SET PLAY

Five options exist out of this set designed for the closing seconds.

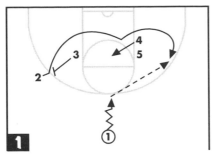

DIAGRAM 1: The first option is 2 coming off the single screen, then 3 after setting the screen. 2 off the double screen is the third option.
DIAGRAM 2: The fourth option is 4, flashing to the middle.
DIAGRAM 3: The fifth option is 5 crossing the lane to the low post.

—Steven M. Garber, Florence, S.C.

GAME WINNER

This quick hitter has a scoring option for each player, works best against a man-to-man defense and has indeed won games for us.

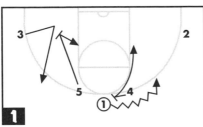

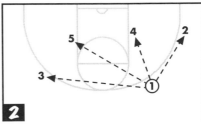

DIAGRAM 1: 1 and 4 execute the screen and roll, initiated by 4's high ball screen. 2 stays in the ball side corner. 3 walks their defender toward the lane and cuts off 5's down screen.

DIAGRAM 2: The five scoring options in order of frequency are: 1-jumper off the screen or drive to the basket; 4-layup or short jumper off the roll after screening; 2-corner jump shot; 5-open and duck into the lane after screening; 3-jumper off the screen from 5.

—Dave Frohman,
Dickinson College, Carlisle, Pa.

"KNOCKOUT": A LAST POSSESSION THREE-POINT SHOT

This play called "Knockout" is run for 2.

DIAGRAM 1: 1 dribbles off a high screen by 5 on the side of 2. 2 then cuts the baseline behind 4. 3 picks down on 2's defender.

DIAGRAM 2: After setting the pick for 1, 5 waits for the play to develop. 5 then goes over and sets a pick, or "cleans up," on any defender who might switch onto 2. 2 pops out beyond the three-point arc for 1's skip pass and a three-point shot.

—David Hoch,
Eastern Technical High School,
Baltimore, Md.

LAST SECOND SHOT FOR A SCORE

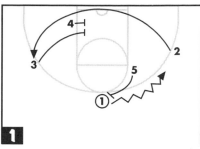

DIAGRAM 1: 5 sets a ball screen for 1. 2 runs off a double screen set by 3 and 4.

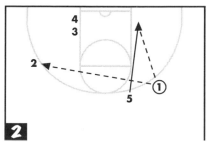

DIAGRAM 2: 5 and 1 execute a screen and roll. If this is stopped, 1 will look to skip to 2 for a shot.

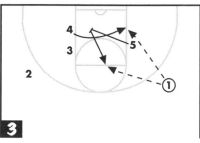

DIAGRAM 3: The final option is 5 cross-screening for 4 and then 5 sealing on the inside.

—Chris Beckman,
Episcopal High School,
Baton Rouge, La.

LAST SHOT AGAINST ZONE

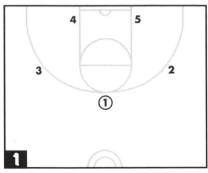

DIAGRAM 1: Initial setup is the 1-2-2. The ball is moved around until only 15 seconds remain in the game, then the call is made to run the play. Attack inside first, unlike many zone theories. Make sure the shot is taken with 6 seconds left.

DIAGRAM 2: 1 passes to 3 and goes toward the pass to create a lane for 3's return pass. 2, the best shooter, stacks under 5.

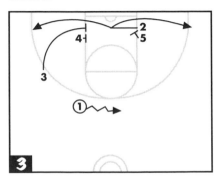

DIAGRAM 3: 3 sets a second screen below 4. 1 dribbles to the middle of the court and reads 2's cut. 2 comes out off 5's screen or the double screen set by 3 and 4.

DIAGRAM 4: 1's first look is to 4 (or 5) on a flash after 2 clears their screens. The final option is 2's jump shot or a jump pass into 4 or 5 in the post.

DIAGRAM 5: If 1 passes to 2 coming off the double screen, 3 clears to the opposite side. 3 clears because there is a double team on the weak side and 4 has the post position alone.

—Pat Sullivan,
College Of St. Francis,
Joliet, Ill.

LATE GAME OPTIONS

This setup for late game situations offers several options.

OPTION 1: A chance to penetrate with your best ball handler (1).

OPTION 2: Two shooters (2 and 3) spotting up in case their defenders help on the penetration.

OPTION 3: A big man (4) who can shoot, making an unusual cut to get open.

OPTION 4: A clear-out situation with no help side for 5.

OPTION 5: Good running rebound position and angles.

—Mack McCarthy, University of Tennessee-Chattanooga, Chattanooga, Tenn.

LATE THREE-POINT SHOT

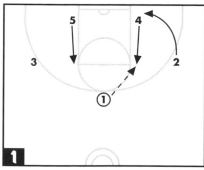

DIAGRAM 1: 4 and 5 flash forward. 1 hits 4. 2 back cuts to the block.

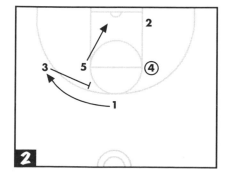

DIAGRAM 2: 3 fade screens for 1. 5 dives to the basket.

DIAGRAM 3: 4 passes to 1. 4 and 3 stagger screen for 2.

—Mack McCarthy,
University of Tennessee-Chattanooga,
Chattanooga, Tenn.

A LAST SECOND HALF-COURT SCORING PLAY

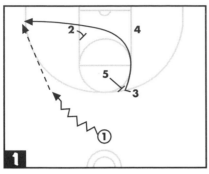

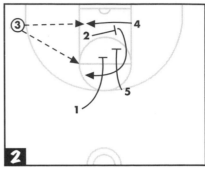

DIAGRAM 1: 1 dribbles to the left as 3 jab-steps, then cuts to the ball side corner off 2's pick. 1 passes to 3.

DIAGRAM 2: 3 hits the corner jumper if open. If not, 3 passes to 4 coming across the lane or 2, who has cut to the top off a double screen by 1 and 5.

—John Gibson, University of Tennessee-Chattanooga, Chattanooga, Tenn.

FULLCOURT PLAYS

PLAY WITH 5 SECONDS REMAINING

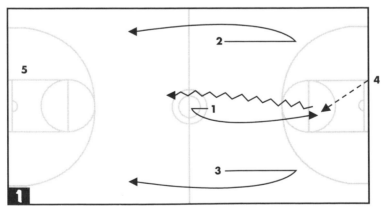

DIAGRAM 1: 4 takes the ball out. 1 fakes long, then comes back for the ball. 2 and 3 fake toward the ball, then break long.

If 4 hits 1, 1 dribbles up the middle of the court looking to pass.

If 4 hits 2 or 3, they should look to center the ball and run the lanes.

5 waits until the ball is across mid-court, then tries to to flash into the lane.

—Mack McCarthy,
Virginia Commonwealth University,
Richmond, Va.

END OF GAME SCORING PLAY

This play is very effective at the end of a game when you need to go the length of the floor with less than 5 seconds to go to tie or win with your opponent playing man-to-man.

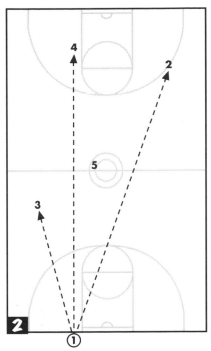

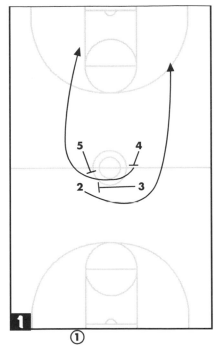

DIAGRAM 1: 2 runs their defender into a staggered screen at midcourt set by 3 and 4. 2 spots up outside the three-point line for a shot.

DIAGRAM 2: 1, the inbounder, must be a good passer because they have to make a baseball pass to 2. If 2 is not open, 1 can look for 4 streaking down the opposite side, off a screen set by 5. If 2 and 4 are both covered, 1 should look to 3 as a safety valve to get the ball inbounds.

—Mark Starns, Bourbon County High School, Paris, Ky.

LATE GAME SIDE OUT FOR A "THREE"

Try this play for a late-game opportunity for a shot off the inbounds pass or a secondary look after the pass.

DIAGRAM 1: 2 down screens for 1. This is false action to initiate the set.

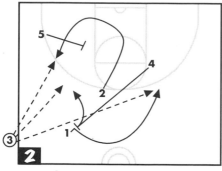

DIAGRAM 2: 2 continues through and curls and fades off 5's screen for one option. 4 back screens for 1, who flare cuts. If passing to 1, 3 must throw the ball to the open spot with a little touch to allow 1 to catch and shoot. 4 slips the screen, looking to catch and shoot.
DIAGRAM 3: Secondary action (with sufficient time remaining)—4 steps out on the slip. 2 back screens inbounder and 1 down screens for 5. 4 dribble penetrates and kicks to either 3 or 5.

Note: As with all plays, put your personnel in the positions here that best fit their skills.

—Stan Jones,
University of Miami,
Coral Gables, Fla.

LATE SECOND SCORING PLAY FROM SIDE OUT

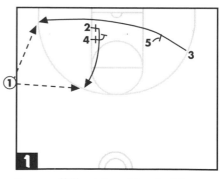

3 runs off 5's pick and the double screen from 2 and 4 to the corner. When 3 clears to the corner, 4 sets a screen for 2, who breaks to the top for the pass from 1. The three options are 2 coming to the top, 3 in the corner and 4 posting up after the screens.

—Allen Carden,
Northwest Whitfield High School,
Tunnell Hill, Ga.

SPECIAL PLAY FOR A LATE GAME "THREE"

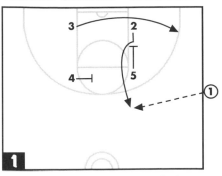

DIAGRAM 1: Working out of a box set with 1 as the inbounder, 2 (your best shooter) comes to the top off 5's down screen to get the inbounds pass. At the same time, 3 cuts through on the baseline to create a triangle with 2 and 5.

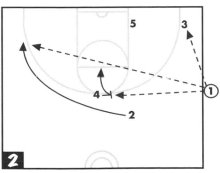

DIAGRAM 2: If 2 doesn't get the pass in, 4 flare screens for 2 and can cut to the basket if their defender helps on 2. The inbounder (1) reads the defense and looks for 3 for a three-pointer on the near side or 2 with a skip pass beyond the arc on the opposite side. 4 also may be open for a "three" up top.

—Seth Greenberg,
Long Beach State University,
Long Beach, Calif.

LAST SECOND SCORING PLAY

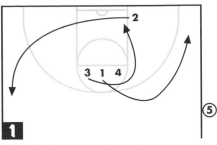

This play has worked for us in games where we needed to score with 4 seconds left. 5 is the inbounder. 3 curls from the foul line to the basket. If 4's defender does not switch, 3 will be able to get two points immediately. If the player guarding 4 does switch, that leaves 4 open for a jump shot. 1 goes to the ball, then fades to the corner. 2 goes from down low across the lane to the opposite side high.

—Michael Ortiz,
Western Samar, Philippines

LAST SECOND INBOUNDS PLAY

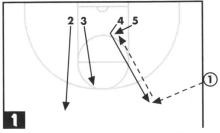

1 passes to hard-flashing 4. 2 and 3 are decoys (and safeties, if needed). After 1 passes to 4, 5 ducks into the lane and gets the pass from 4. 5 takes an easy shot from the lane.

—Jon Pye,
Central Missouri State,
Warrensburg, Mo.

LAST SECOND SIDELINE OUT-OF-BOUNDS WITH TWO OPTIONS

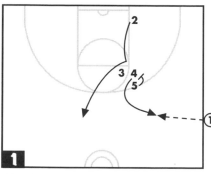

DIAGRAM 1: 1 (your best scorer) takes the ball out-of-bounds. 2 comes off the double screen by 3 and 4, then 4 comes off the screen by 5. 1 inbounds to 4.

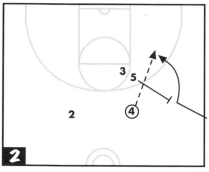

DIAGRAM 2: After the pass in, 1 cuts off 5's back screen and receives the pass back from 4.

—Rich Zvosec,
University of North Florida,
Jacksonville, Fla.

LAST SECOND PLAY VS. ZONE

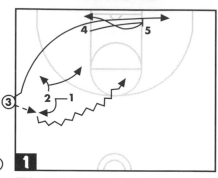

This play is best run after a timeout so that everything can be set. 3 (best baseline shooter) inbounds the ball. 1 and 2 (guards) stack in a straight line and move to get open when 3 slaps the ball. 4 and 5 position at the low post, with 4 being your best rebounder and 5 being your best inside offensive player. 3 inbounds to either guard. 4 slides away and forms a double screen with 5. 3 cuts off this screen. The guard who received the pass from 3 tries to gap-dribble or freeze-dribble the defensive guards by going right at them penetrating as deep as possible, looking for: a shot, 3 coming off the double screen, 5 on a quick flash, 4 sliding across the lane or a quick reversal back to 2. If 1 passes to 3, then 3 looks to either shoot or pass inside to 5.

—Tommy Eagles,
Louisiana Tech University,
Ruston, La.

LAST SECOND SCORING CHANCE

This play can be used as a last second scoring opportunity.

DIAGRAM 1: Have your best all-around player (3) cut around the key getting a screen from all the other players on the floor. 3 should get the pass in stride.

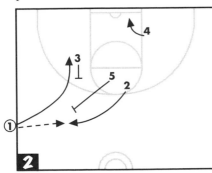

DIAGRAM 2: If 3 is not open then 2 will come back to the ball with 3 and 5 setting screens for 1 to cut to the basket. 4 flashes the post.

—Rich Ward,
University of Maine-Machias,
Machias, Maine

A LATE GAME OUT-OF-BOUNDS SCORING PLAY

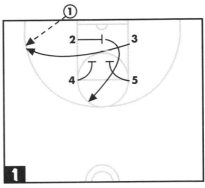

DIAGRAM 1: 1 prepares to inbound the ball, 2 screens for 3 (your best player). 4 and 5 set a double screen for 2 to go to the top of the key.

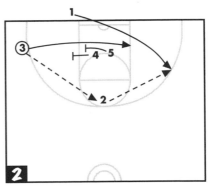

DIAGRAM 2: After inbounding the ball, 1 goes out wide. 3 reverses the ball to 2, who passes to 1. 4 and 5 set a stagger pick for 3 to cut to the ball side block.

—John Gibson,
University of Tennessee-Chattanooga,
Chattanooga, Tenn.

LAST SECOND SIDELINE OUT-OF-BOUNDS PLAY

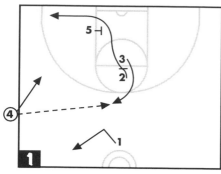

3 comes off the high post stack to receive the ball from 4. 1 V-cuts to get open near halfcourt. After screening for 3, 2 goes off the low block screen set by 5 to flatten out on the baseline. 5 now posts on the block.

4 looks to inbound to 3 first, then to either 1 or 2. 3 catches the ball at the top of the key, with the right side of the floor isolated for a drive to the basket. 3 also looks for 2 cutting, 5 posting or 4 stepping in after inbounding, to take the shot.

If 1 catches the inbounds pass, 1 drives off a ball screen by 3. 3 can either roll or step back off the screen.

—Bill Schmidt,
Oak Hill Academy,
Mouth of Wilson, Va.

LAST SECOND SIDE-LINE OUT-OF-BOUNDS

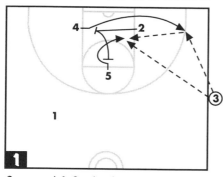

2 sets a pick for 4, who goes to the opposite corner and receives a pass from 3. 2 then picks for 5, who can get the ball from 4; or, if 4 does not have the ball, 5 can receive it directly from 3. After the second pick, 2 can turn toward the ball and receive a pass.

—Gary Edwards,
Charleston Southern University,
Charleston, S.C.

LAST SECOND SHOT

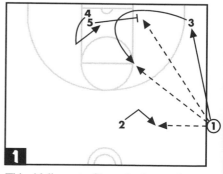

This sideline out-of-bounds play works against either the man-to-man or zone defense. 1 enters to 2 (point guard), 3 at the elbow or 5 on the block. If defense is man-to-man, 4 may be open for a back door lob. After 1 enters the ball, 1 runs to the corner looking for the return pass. ***Man-to-man key:*** Get the ball to 3 and set up a double low post. ***Zone key:*** Get the ball to 3, and 1 is always open in the corner.

—Patrick J. Flannery,
Drexel University,
Philadelphia, Pa.

LAST SECOND PLAY (FIVE OPTIONS)

Try to get the ball on the right side of the floor, since most players are right-handed and prefer going to the right as this play develops. 3 inbounds; 5, 4 and 2 are set diagonally across the elbow facing midcourt. 1 is on the weak side.

OPTION A: On 3's slap, 5 takes a step toward the midline and turns to go off the double screen by 2 and 4, who have stepped up.

OPTION B: 4 turns quickly to screen for 2, who looks for the shot going right toward the corner.

OPTION C: 4 follows 2 and also looks for the shot going right.

OPTION D: 1 cuts to the ball for a top of the key shot.

OPTION E: If 4 gets the ball right after the screen for 2, 1 may drop

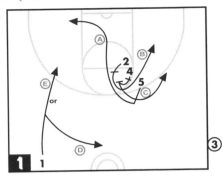

down the weak side and break for a quick pass from 4.

In all cases, 5 looks for a tip-in, depending on the time left.

—Bob Valvano,
St. Francis College,
Brooklyn, N.Y.

LAST SECOND INBOUNDS: TWO OPTIONS

1 passes to hard-flashing 4. 2 and 3 are decoys (and safeties, if needed). After 1 passes to 4, 5 ducks into the lane, then turns out to headhunt 1's defender for a back pick.

OPTION 1: 1 uses the back pick to go to the basket for the pass from 4.

OPTION 2: If 1 is not open on 5's back pick, 5 rolls to the hoop for the pass from 4 and a 10- or 12-foot shot.

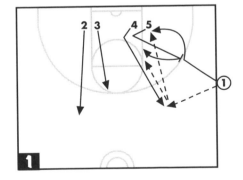

—Jon Pye, Central Missouri State, Warrensburg, Mo.

Chapter 8

MISCELLANEOUS "GIMIC" PLAYS

THREE TIP PLAYS

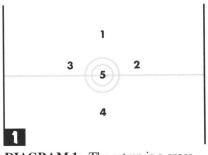

1

DIAGRAM 1: The set up is a cross. Use this play if you have control of the tip. The biggest forward is 1. The center is 5. The best defensive guard is 4. The other team can prevent a layup out of this setup, but it cannot prevent you from controlling the tip. The key to the tip is to have your center enter the jump circle last and see which way to tip before entering.

2

DIAGRAM 2: This is a box set up. Use this if the percentage that you will win the tip is 50 percent. Always try to establish inside position.

3

DIAGRAM 3: This is the triangle set up. If you know the other team will control the tip, prevent the easy layup with this formation. 4 is your best defensive player.

With the advent of the possession arrow, these plays are not as valuable early in the game as they are in over-time.

—Frank Messenger,
Elizabeth High School,
Elizabeth, Colo.

FIVE-POINT DEFENSIVE DRILL

This drill is effective because it incorporates five separate concepts: wing denial, jumping to the ball, playing the flash cut, help and recover and closing out.

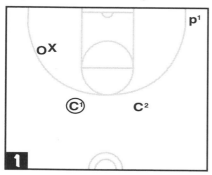

DIAGRAM 1: C1 has the ball. O is on offense working to get open on the wing, X denies on the wing.

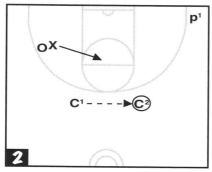

DIAGRAM 2: C1 passes to C2. X must move away from his or her player and move into the help position.

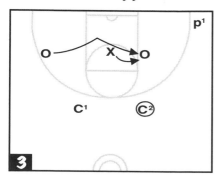

DIAGRAM 3: After a slight pause, O flashes to the mid-post area. X must beat O to the spot and deny the post feed.

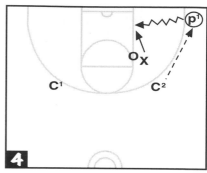

DIAGRAM 4: C2 passes to P1 behind the three-point line. P1 drives the baseline. X must shut off the baseline and take the charge.

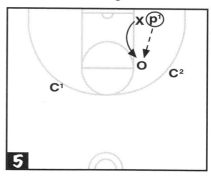

DIAGRAM 5: After X shuts off the baseline, P1 passes to O at the elbow. X must recover and close on O, who tries to score in the one-on-one situation.

—Steve Schulman,
Binghamton University,
Binghamton, N.Y.

THE PRINCETON MAN-TO-MAN PRESS BREAK

The Princeton man press break has solved my problems against tough man-to-man pressing teams. It's easy to set up and easier to execute. Each player should have specific skills and attributes, as follows: 1-best ball handling guard; 2 (center)-best screener; 3 (guard)-good ball handler; 4-larger forward; 5 (forward)-best ball handling big man.

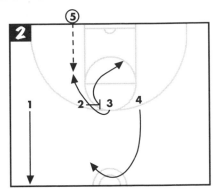

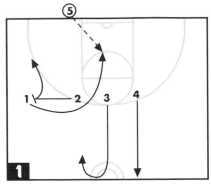

DIAGRAM 1: As 5 inbounds the ball, 4 goes deep. 3 goes to the half-court circle. 2 screens for 1 and rolls to the opposite side. 1 comes off the screen to the pass.

DIAGRAM 2: 4 goes to the half-court circle. 2 screens for 3 and rolls opposite. 3 comes off the screen to the pass. 1 goes deep.

These are our two basic plays; you can also change assignments for any of the players on the court at any time.

—Steve Lasman,
Sedan High School,
Sedan, Kan.

PLAY FOR CENTER JUMP BREAK

On the toss of the ball, 5 tips the ball back to 3. 1 and 2 break out to the side line. 3 passes to either 1 or 2 and 5 breaks to the basket as 4 steps up and sets a back screen for 5. 2 (the roles of 1 and 2 are interchangeable) dribbles down the side line and looks for 5. 1 fills the lane on the opposite side.

—Andrew DeGregrio,
Queens, N.Y.

MISSED FREE-THROW PLAY

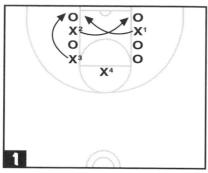

Sometimes it is beneficial to miss a free throw to pull out a victory. To intentionally miss a free throw, X4 shoots a flat free throw, making sure he or she hits the rim. X1 steps across the lane, followed immediately by X2. X3 goes behind X2 looking for a baseline rebound.

—Keith Siefkes,
Beth Eden Baptist School,
Denver, Colo.

SIDELINE PLAY TO START HALF

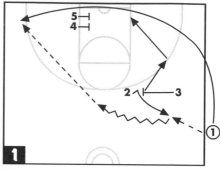

We run this play to start a half for a good look at a three-point shot by our best shooter on the floor.

DIAGRAM 1: 1 passes the ball into 2 or 3. After 1 passes, 1 cuts down the sideline and baseline and uses the double screen set by 4 and 5 to get open for a three-point shot in the corner.

—Bill D. Kunze,
Duluth East High School,
Duluth, Minn.

___ IN THE HOLE

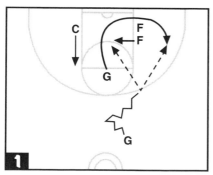

Many teams not as talented as their opponents may wish to run the clock down to 12 or 15 seconds before taking a shot. The problem with this strategy is, what kind of shot do I get with only 12 to 15 seconds? And what if the defense changes?

So we run what is called, "___ in the Hole." The "___" is some player's name. That person runs off the single or double screen. Note the way the double screen breaks up, allowing us to go to the middle for an easy shot.

—Tom Smith, Valparaiso University, Valparaiso, Ind.

THE SHOOTING DRILL

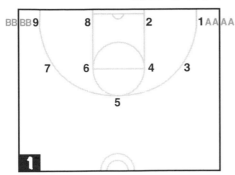

DIAGRAM 1: This is a shooting drill that takes only a few minutes and the players love it.

Use nine spots as shown. The more balls you use, the quicker the drill goes. Players line up behind the 1 and 9 spots.

On a signal, the first person in each line shoots from the same spot. On a made basket, the next player in line moves to the next spot.

Each team must make it through all nine spots and then back again.

The first team that hits from the spot at which it began is declared the winner.

—Bill Miller,
Moira Secondary School,
Belleville, Ontario, Canada

GLOSSARY OF TERMS

(Note: Positional descriptions can vary based on players.)

BALL HANDLER—The player who dribbles and runs the offense.

BALL SIDE—The side of the court where the ball is located.

BASELINE—The line at either end of the court that runs parallel to the backboard. Can describe players' motion toward the baseline in offensive movement.

BLOCK—The portion of the free-throw lane nearest the baseline.

CENTER—Usually the tallest player on a team.

CUTTER—Player who moves off a screen toward the basket or to receive a pass.

FAST BREAK—An offensive strategy in which a team advances the ball quickly up the court to score an easy basket.

FIELD GOAL—A successful attempt at a shot.

FORWARD—A player who is usually tall and can shoot from the perimeter and rebound.

FREE THROW—A 15-foot shot taken from the foul line.

FREE-THROW LINE—A line 15 feet from the basket behind which players take free throws.

FREE-THROW LINE EXTENDED—A parallel position extended to the right or left of the free throw line by a few feet.

HELP SIDE—Opposite the ball.

HIGH POST—The area around and near the free-throw line.

INBOUNDS PASS—Throwing the ball in play from out of bounds.

HOOK SHOT—Offensive set shot during which the player turns his or her body sideways and arcs a ball in the air toward the basket. Usually done by a forward or center.

JUMP SHOT—An attempt from the floor to make a basket, usually from more than 5 feet away from the basket.

LAYUP—A shot from very close range, usually as a player dribbles directly at the basket.

LOW POST—Area along the free-throw line.

MAN-TO-MAN—Each player is assigned the responsibility of playing against one specific player from the other team.

OUT OF BOUNDS—Outside the playing area. The area from which a pass can be made to bring the ball into the area of play.

PERIMETER—Outside the free-throw lane.

PIVOT FOOT—Offensive player must keep this foot in contact with the floor at all times when not dribbling.

POINT GUARD—Primary ballhandler in the offense.

POST—Area along the free-throw lane and halfway up the lane toward the free-throw line.

PRESS—When the defense extends pressure to the half-court line (half-court press), to the free-throw line (three-quarters press) or to the baseline (full-court press).

SCREEN—An offensive player intentionally blocks the path of a defensive player.

SCREENER—An offensive player who blocks the path of a teammate's defensive player.

STRONG SIDE—Side of the court where the ball is located.

THREE-POINT LINE—Semicircle that runs around the perimeter of the basket and from beyond which a basket worth three points is attempted.

THREE-POINT SHOT—Shot from beyond the three-point line.

TOP OF THE KEY—Area slightly beyond the top of the free-throw lane.

WEAK SIDE—Area of the court opposite the ball.

WING—Area to the side of the offensive setup, usually the free-throw line toward the sideline.

ZONE—When players are assigned a certain area to play instead of a certain player to play.